A John Steinbeck Reader

Essays in Honor of Stephen K. George

Edited by Barbara A. Heavilin

THE SCARECROW PRESS, INC.
Lanham, MD • Toronto • Plymouth, UK
2009

SCARECROW PRESS, INC.

Published in the United States of America
by Scarecrow Press, Inc.
A wholly owned subsidiary of
The Rowman & Littlefield Publishing Group, Inc.
4501 Forbes Boulevard, Suite 200, Lanham, Maryland 20706
www.scarecrowpress.com

Estover Road
Plymouth PL6 7PY
United Kingdom

British Library Cataloguing in Publication Information Available

Library of Congress Cataloging-in-Publication Data

A John Steinbeck reader : essays in honor of Stephen K. George / edited by
Barbara A. Heavilin.
    p. cm.
  Includes bibliographical references and index.
  ISBN-13: 978-0-8108-6699-7 (pbk. : alk. paper)
  ISBN-10: 0-8108-6699-4 (pbk. : alk. paper)
  ISBN-13: 978-0-8108-6712-3 (e-book)
  ISBN-10: 0-8108-6712-5 (e-book)
  1. Steinbeck, John, 1902–1968—Criticism and interpretation.
2. Steinbeck, John, 1902–1968—Characters. 3. Steinbeck, John, 1902–
1968—Appreciation. 4. Politics and literature. I. Heavilin, Barbara A.,
1945–. II. George, Stephen K., 1965–.
PS3537.T3234Z715496 2009
813'.52—dc22   2008042012

♾™ The paper used in this publication meets the minimum requirements
of American National Standard for Information Sciences—Permanence of
Paper for Printed Library Materials, ANSI/NISO Z39.48-1992.
Manufactured in the United States of America.

In memory of Stephen K. George,
husband, father, friend, colleague, and scholar

Set me like a seal on your heart,
like a seal on your arm.
For love is strong as death.
—The Song of Songs 7:6, *The Jerusalem Bible*

Contents

Foreword

In Memory of Stephen K. George

John H. Timmerman
Calvin College

Writing a foreword to a collection of scholarly works may seem to some a task as arid as a desert sand, as interesting as fog. Such is not the case here. The much harder challenge is how we, as fellow scholars, do justice to the memory of one of our brightest lights. I think this collection achieves that task. Individually, the articles represent intelligent and insightful scholarship. Collectively, they celebrate the lively intellect and caring spirit of Stephen K. George, whose life on this earth ended on November 1, 2006, at the age of 41.

Stephen has left behind a legacy for us Steinbeck scholars, especially with his seemingly boundless energy and vision. More importantly he left behind a legacy for his family, community, and students at Brigham Young University–Idaho. A vacancy will always exist for his wife Rebecca and their six children—each one named after a Jane Austen character (Louisa, Emma, Margaret, Henry, Charles, and Elizabeth). Rebecca remembers him as a "true Renaissance man," one who equally loved sports and great art, particularly music. If Stephen was a Renaissance man, however, he was first of all a man of deep integrity and genuine character.

His students also testified to these traits, noting that while Stephen was a recognized scholar, with many publications, he was first of all concerned with their thoughts and work. Perhaps in these days of the furious swirl we are losing contact with that good old word *respect*. In its Latin root the word signified something earned, not sought or demanded. It is a word often used by those who spent much time around Stephen. In *Fear and Trembling*, Soren Kierkegaard set out to define his Knight of Faith and observes at one point: "The true knight of faith is a witness, never a teacher, and therein lies his deep humanity." In Kierkegaard's estimation, witnesses testify to the truth they hold dear by their actions; teachers profess only facts accumulated. The respect paid to Stephen derived in no small measure from his personal witness.

We are, perhaps, best acquainted with Stephen's scholarly activities. They started early. In his introduction to *John Steinbeck: A Centennial Tribute*, Stephen recalls how they began to focus on Steinbeck: "On a cold December afternoon in 1986, with the snow gently falling outside, I began reading a worn copy of *The Grapes of Wrath* on a sofa in my cramped student apartment. I didn't stop until daybreak the next day—it was the most powerful reading experience of my college years." That singular event charted a course for future years. It also led him to study for his Ph.D. at Ball State University, home to one of the nation's leading Steinbeck collections. There he also met and studied with Tetsumaro (Ted) Hayashi, one of the founding scholars of modern Steinbeck studies. Stephen's doctoral thesis critically assessed the ethics of *Of Mice and Men*, an approach that Stephen pursued often in later years.

In short order Stephen edited or co-edited three major volumes of Steinbeck criticism—*John Steinbeck: A Centennial Tribute*; *The Moral Philosophy of John Steinbeck*; and *John Steinbeck and His Contemporaries*—as well as dozens of articles and reviews. At the time of his death, Stephen was co-editor of the *Steinbeck Review* and co-director of the Steinbeck Society of America.

Stephen George left behind a spirit of sound scholarship, a devotion to painstaking and yet gentle care of his professional duties, and a visionary sense of Steinbeck studies that unified us all. He was a rare person, the very best of his kind; indeed, he was a Renaissance man with a humanitarian spirit.

It is my fondest wish that these essays might honor his memory, and also his love for Rebecca and the six young Austens. May their own stories grow rich every day in the light of their father's love and honor.

Preface

Barbara A. Heavilin

> A third generation of Steinbeck scholars and readers now carry his torch, finding in the work of this writer a philosophical probing, an artistic craftsmanship, a courage and compassion that make his books come alive despite a twenty-first-century audience's distance from the Great Depression, World War II, and John F. Kennedy's assassination. There is something self-evident about a writer who can touch a lad in London, a Catholic in Chicago, a Japanese reader in Kyoto, and, in my case, a kid from backwoods Kentucky for whom California was another world. John Steinbeck captures the minds and hearts of his readers and continues to inspire today. What more do we require?
>
> —Stephen K. George in *John Steinbeck: A Centennial Tribute*

I have come to regard *A John Steinbeck Reader: Essays in Honor of Stephen K. George* as the end of a journey begun several years ago in 1993 at a Steinbeck conference I directed at Taylor University, where I met a smiling young Steinbeck scholar with a soft Southern drawl. Stephen was a member of Dr. Tetsumaro Hayashi's Steinbeck seminar at Ball State University, which was in attendance that day. When he began his university teaching, he invited me to present a paper on a panel he was getting together for the Steinbeck conference at Hofstra. I invited him to join me as co-editor of the *Steinbeck Yearbook*. Together, we created a new journal, the *Steinbeck Review*, that was less expensive and more accessible to scholars than the *Yearbook* had been. And we began the editing of *John Steinbeck and His Contemporaries* together even though he was in the final stages of his courageous battle with colon cancer. The e-mails were exchanged even up to the week he died. Such was his rock-solid commitment to a task to be done and a vision to be fulfilled.

Neither of us received released time from our universities for this research, writing, and editing. Evenings, weekends, holidays, summer vacations—both of us took from these personal times to devote to scholarly tasks. Both of us found joy in the work and in our work together. A rare person of magnanimity, Stephen, figuratively speaking, put his arms around the globe, encouraging Steinbeck scholars from places as far flung as Slovenia, Belgium, Africa, Japan, China, and Korea. It was vitally important to him that *John Steinbeck and His Contemporaries* should be global in scope and representation, and that the *Steinbeck Review* include those scholars outside the borders of the United States. And I believe that both do. It was important to him as well that the Steinbeck community—long divided by strife and turf guarding—should become united and focused on the goal of furthering Steinbeck scholarship in what he termed "a new spirit of collegiality and good will." This community is certainly approaching that goal. It was his dream that Steinbeck scholarship continue to broaden in perspective, and he suggested several avenues for further study—interdisciplinary, comparative, aesthetic, and pedagogical. This goal also is being fulfilled, even in the present book.

I believe he would be pleased with *A John Steinbeck Reader*. In its preparation, I kept having the uncanny feeling that he was watching over its production, as had been our custom of checking over one another's work and accomplishments in the past. I know he would be pleased with the representation of old friends, colleagues, and scholars—John Timmerman, Luchen Li, Michael Meyer, Tetsumaro Hayashi, Mimi Gladstein, among others. And he would be pleased with its international representation—Japan's Kyoshi Nakayama and Slovenia's Danica Cerce. He would like, too, the book's range of scholarly perspective—from aesthetics, to ethics, to cultural, among other approaches. Stephen's life was all too short, but his accomplishments compare well with those of scholars who were granted many more years than he had on this earth. A man of passion for

Steinbeck studies, of love for his family and colleagues, of generous and sacrificial spirit, he has left us with an enduring legacy of good scholarship and good will. As he writes of his beloved Steinbeck, "What more do we require?"

WORK CITED

George, Stephen K. "Crossing the Oceans: The Future of Steinbeck Studies in America, Japan, and Beyond." *Steinbeck Review and Steinbeck Studies.* Vol. 3, No. 1, 105.

Acknowledgments

Barbara A. Heavilin

To my essay readers, John H. Timmerman and Mary M. Brown, and to my husband, Charles—my strongest critic and supporter—I am most grateful. Copyright acknowledgement is made for the use of the following:

- Stephen K. George's "The Contemporary Nature of Steinbeck's Winter: Artistry, Integrity, and September 11" from *Steinbeck Yearbook*, Volume III, 2003, ed. Barbara A. Heavilin and Stephen K. George, 65–79, with the permission of The Edwin Mellen Press.
- Michael Meyer's "It's All in Your Head: Transforming Heavenly and Hellish Settings in Steinbeck's *The Pastures of Heaven*" from *Steinbeck Yearbook*, Volume III, 2003, ed. Barbara A. Heavilin and Stephen K. George, 81–104, with the permission of The Edwin Mellen Press.
- Cover photo of John Steinbeck in Prague, Czechoslovakia, 1947, used by courtesy of the Martha Heasley Cox Center for Steinbeck Studies, San Jose State University.

Introduction

Barbara A. Heavilin

A work of art that enters us to feed the soul offers to initiate in us the process of the gifted self which some antecedent gift initiated in the poet. Reading the work, *we* feel gifted for a while, and to the degree that we are able, we respond by creating new work (not art, perhaps, but with the artist's work at hand we suddenly find we can make sense of our own experience).

> —Lewis Hyde, *The Gift: Imagination and the Erotic Life of Property* (1983)

This book celebrates "the process of the gifted self which some antecedent gift initiated in the poet"—a gift that, for a while at least, makes critic and reader "feel gifted" as well. (Poet, of course, is used here in the Aristotelian sense of the imaginative writer.) It brings to Steinbeck scholarship a varied array of aesthetic and critical approaches—ranging from Mary Brown's poetic interpretation of Mary Hawley from *The Winter of Our Discontent* and Thom Satterlee's dialogue with Lee from *East of Eden* in "Part I: Poetic Views of Two Steinbeck Characters," to critical approaches from the aesthetic to the cultural, to a meditative reading of a rarely read early short story, and more.

"Part 2: Steinbeck, Aesthetics, and Ethics" focuses on art in the interest of societal and ecological ethics. As its title implies, Stephen

George's "The Contemporary Nature of Steinbeck's *Winter*: Artistry, Integrity, and September 11" delves into aesthetics and ethics in what was probably his favorite Steinbeck work, maintaining that it is "one of Steinbeck's finest and most daring novels," speaking

> directly to . . . core issues. It not only explores the depths of individual and societal corruption with its vanguard use of setting and postmodern narrative technique, it offers insight into the means for our redemption. *Winter*—like *Hamlet*, the Bible, and Dante's *Inferno*—is a work whose theme is for the ages. A contemporary audience would be wise to listen lest its final words prove true and another light goes out.

Barbara Heavilin's "'Only through Imitation Do We Develop towards Originality': Reflections of Joseph Addison's *Spectator* in Steinbeck's *Travels with Charley*" goes back to Steinbeck's literary roots, deep in eighteenth-century British literature. She finds that by imitating Addison's style and

> sharing his roles as thinker, social critic, and observer of humankind, he emerges as Mr. American Spectator—a kindly relative of Addison's British Mr. Spectator and his keen observations of the London scene in his newspaper. Both writers are lovers of humanity, with faith in humankind's capacity for perfection.

Steinbeck's "originality" at least in *Travels with Charley*, then, owes much to this British writer.

While George finds in Steinbeck's final novel, *Winter*, some "insight into the means for our redemption" and advises "a contemporary audience . . . to listen lest its final words prove true and another light goes out," John Timmerman's "Charley, America, and Malory: John Steinbeck's Later Ethics" takes a bleaker stance on Steinbeck's later vision in *America and Americans*, maintaining that

> in the ever-depressing and devolving litany of failure articulated in *America and Americans*, Steinbeck oddly places his optimism in humanity. . . . Essentially, Steinbeck's ethics in *America* is thoroughly postmodern and relativist. Our strength and salvation arises from within ourselves. . . . The ethical problem should be readily apparent. Who is to say whose strength is right or wrong? Steinbeck laments the passing of the old virtues and codes of conduct, but says little about how to establish new ones. Against the waning of Camelot into the glooming dark, Steinbeck finds few bulwarks except an optimistic faith in humanity itself.

Sadly, Timmerman's comments apply to *Winter* as well. Hawley is a frail light bearer at best, and Steinbeck gives no indication as to what kind of civic leader he will now become. Having dismantled his ethical moorings once, might he not do so again?

The two essays in "Part 3: Steinbeck, the Child's View, and Lonely Ladies"—the one focusing on the writer's authentic portrayal of children and the other a comparative study of lonely women in short stories by Steinbeck and Cather—reveal Steinbeck's empathic creation of character. Mimi Gladstein's "Through the Eyes of a Child: A Steinbeck Forte" finds that Steinbeck

> was able to invoke a sense of his boyhood, delve into his immature memory banks and create children who ring true. Steinbeck's children are sentient creatures who experience and think about the world as children, thus appealing to the child in the reader.

And in "Lonely Ladies and Landscapes: A Comparison of John Steinbeck's 'The White Quail' and Eudora Welty's 'A Curtain of Green,'" Charlotte Hadella maintains that the "varied implementation of the 'woman as garden' motif points to the influence of gender perspectives" in these short stories. Steinbeck explores the male as well as the female perspective, resulting in "major differences between the two authors' social commentary: while 'A Curtain of Green' emphasizes a process of healing by focusing on human *need*, 'The White Quail' focuses on *blame*."

"Part 4: Steinbeck, the American Ideal, Politics, and War" opens with Stephen Tanner's "Steinbeck's *The Winter of Our Discontent* and the American Ideal." Like George and Timmerman, Tanner explores Steinbeck's vision of America, maintaining that the light that must be kept burning is "a distinctively American brand of idealism," based on principles and symbolized in the Hawley family talisman. Ultimately, Tanner states, Ethan is saved by "the talisman and all that it represents." Concerning the novel's aesthetic merit, Tanner concludes, "I would suggest by my formalistic analysis that it is more artistically coherent than is generally acknowledged—it is a unique and unlikely to be emulated investigation of the American ideal under threat."

Danica Cerce's "Art for Politics: The Political Dimension of Steinbeck's Works in Eastern Europe" opens with an intriguing premise:

> Just as it is impossible to neglect the political implications of literary masterpieces and concur with Nietzsche that the aesthetic is the only

justification for the world, as he writes in *The Birth of Tragedy*, so it is wrong to believe, with Levine, that "all things are political," and on the basis of this theory, replace literary studies with cultural or political ones (378–79). However, during the communist era, a genuine work of art was worth at least as much as any major political act.

Her thesis incorporates this premise with text-oriented analysis, presenting "a newly devised set of concepts regarding the creative potential of fictional worlds in communist Eastern Europe."

Tetsumaro Hayashi's "John Steinbeck as Lyndon B. Johnson's Speech Writer" finds that Johnson served as inspiration for "Steinbeck's political awareness, thinking, and writing" and that Steinbeck helped to enforce, focus, and articulate Johnson's "idealistic, political philosophy and . . . develop the means by which to preach the gospel of the Great Society more effectively to the American people."

"Part 5: Steinbeck, Culture, Viewpoints, and a Meditative Reading" opens with Luchen Li's "John Steinbeck's Cultural Frontiers," in which he asserts that "Steinbeck believes that human beings are not just cultural or political or economic animals, but fundamentally a species in nature, a unique and hopeful part of the whole and never detached totally from it." Focusing on the power of the human imagination, Michael J. Meyer's "It's All in Your Head: Transforming Heavenly and Hellish Settings in Steinbeck's *The Pastures of Heaven*" contends that Steinbeck

> believed in the human ability to make heavens out of hells and hells out of heavens—at least for a moment or two. The theme of the power of the human mind, celebrated by both Milton and Shakepeare, reappears in *The Pastures of Heaven*, as Steinbeck reworks old perceptions and presents them in a new way.

In "The Short, Happy Life of *Pippin IV*: The Grand Joke," Brian Railsback compares Steinbeck's approach to his art with that of Hemingway and traces the inception and critical history of *Pippin IV*, concluding that Steinbeck

> looked upon the short, happy life of *Pippin* as the grand joke that it was meant to be. He would have likely told the critics of the future that they should peruse the aisles for *The Grapes of Wrath* or *Cannery Row* if they wished, but that a book like *The Short Reign of Pippin IV* did not deserve a place on the shelves at all.

The book's final essay, "'Fingers of Cloud: A Satire on College Protervity': A Meditative Reading," by Kyoshi Nakayama has a section on Steinbeck's combining the fantastic and the realistic that one of the readers for this book found especially intriguing: "The points Nakayama raises about that combining and about American prejudices do for me what Fran Rippy used to teach us all good criticism does—send us back to the literature. I'm really very interested in reading and considering this story further." As Lewis Hyde suggests, reading is a work of art—and even the critic's response to that art may initiate in us "the gifted self which some antecedent gift initiated in the poet." It is my hope that this book further perpetuates this gift.

Part 1

POETIC VIEWS OF TWO STEINBECK CHARACTERS

I'm looking forward to the sweet scent of good thinking.

—Thom Satterlee

I propose a toast to immortality through words. What shall we drink?

—Thom Satterlee

1

Contented—for Mary Hawley

(And, in Another Way, for Stephen George)

Mary M. Brown
Indiana Wesleyan University

Perhaps you too have kept a private place, a cave,
a closet, present tense, a yolk opaque and warm
as stone. Perhaps the girl in you is woman too,
first person human being, tough as boot—with

what's-so-good-about-it-Friday dark and deep
beneath your boat of resurrection—bold swash-
buckling pilgrim, freewheeling prophet preaching
liberty and gospel to the many cans of beans.

Perhaps in the middle of your sweet seeming
sleep you too have secret dreams in which
you clobber children, rob a ship, a bank, betray
a husband, closest friend, revert to baser genes.

So in the morning you can lie content beside
the funny man who calls you *wiggles, pin curl, flower feet.*

2

A Dialogue with Steinbeck's Lee Concerning Servanthood, *Timshel*, and Immortality through Words

Thom Satterlee
Taylor University

I know we'll never meet in person, so I propose we meet here, in words.

I'm looking forward to the sweet smell of good thinking.

I am, too. But I worry. I worry about misrepresenting you.

I'm a servant. I'm old. I'm Chinese.

I know these things. But you're more, too.

My father clawed me out of the tattered meat of my mother. She died on the shale in the afternoon.

That's what I mean—you insist on the truth.

Even if it is a dreadful truth. My parents, my dear parents.

I think you're the most complex and interesting character in all of Steinbeck's work. I'm afraid to get you wrong.

Is it responsibility or blame that bothers you? Sometimes responsibility is worse. It doesn't carry any pleasant egotism.

Egotism is exactly what I'm trying to get rid of. I thought you, as a servant, would teach me.

I never saw anybody get so mixed up in other people's business the way I do.

Tell me again what it means to be a servant.

I don't know where being a servant came into disrepute. Properly carried out, it is a position of power, even love.

Yes, the way you put it makes servanthood sound attractive.

A servant loses his initiative.

I recall you said that, too.

I'm crotchety. I feel sand under my skin.

I don't understand why—not if being a servant leads, as you say, to power and love.

Haven't you heard of all Chinese servants that when they get old they remain loyal but they turn mean?

Perhaps meanness is necessary in order to serve. You would have fought Aron to do him and his father good.

Thank heaven that's over.

You even swore at him, a minister wannabe!

I am not profane by accident.

My point exactly. I think you are a thoroughgoing servant. You adapt yourself, finally, to what the other person needs. Adam, Cal, Aron, Abra, and I—we all need you.

Please try not to need me. That's the worst bait of all to a lonely man. I'm too closely married to a reading lamp.

I know you love books. And I know your favorite word . . .

Timshel—thou mayest.

Exactly.

"Thou mayest"—that gives a choice. It might be the most important word in the world.

Yes. Adam needs that word. Cal needs it, too. And you found it for them—you and your ancestors reading Hebrew and parsing its meaning.

You should have sat through some of those nights of argument and discussion. The questions, the inspection, oh, the lovely thinking—the beautiful thinking. Those old men are critics of truth.

And so are you, Lee. You're a servant of truth. That's why, at the last page, I begin to miss you.

I hope I'm not so small-souled as to take satisfaction in being missed.

I'd be smaller souled without you. I grow in proportion to how well I understand you.

You can only understand people if you feel them in yourself.

And so I feel you. The closer I draw to your words, the more alive and real you seem.

Maybe that's what immortality is.

Do you really believe that?

Yes I believe it, and you'd better believe it.

Then I will. I propose a toast to immortality through words. What shall we drink?

Chinee blandy. Stlong dlink.

Ah, ng-ka-py! And you'll pour it from your stone jug into the thin porcelain cups? Perfect.

It's my own invention.

Lee, I hope I haven't said anything here that offended you.

You should say anything you want.

Then you enjoyed our dialogue? You're not disturbed?

Let the ng-ka-py run back on your tongue.

It tastes like rotten apples.

Like good rotten apples.

Part 2

STEINBECK, AESTHETICS, AND ETHICS

In the ever-depressing and devolving litany of failure articulated in *America and Americans*, Steinbeck oddly places his optimism in humanity. One finds a sense of Hegelian progress—out of dialectic we can't go back and we do stumble, sometimes unwittingly, along a road called the future. Essentially, Steinbeck's ethics in *America* is thoroughly postmodern and relativist. Our strength and salvation arises from within ourselves. It had better, or we are doomed. The ethical problem should be readily apparent. Who is to say whose strength is right or wrong? Steinbeck laments the passing of the old virtues and codes of conduct, but says little about how to establish new ones. Against the waning of Camelot into the glooming dark, Steinbeck finds few bulwarks except an optimistic faith in humanity itself.

—John H. Timmerman

3

The Contemporary Nature of Steinbeck's *Winter*

Artistry, Integrity, and September 11

Stephen K. George
Brigham Young University–Idaho

The father of Steinbeck studies, Peter Lisca, once wrote that *The Winter of Our Discontent* was undeniable evidence of the aesthetic and philosophical failure of the writer's later fiction, that "when Steinbeck abandons his earlier [naturalistic and biological] viewpoint and attempts to project an image of man based on such conventional notions as Christian morality and ethical integrity he cannot seem to say anything significant" (10). Most of the leading Steinbeck scholars of that day concurred, condemning Steinbeck's last novel "for its lack of realism, Ethan for his implausibility, the language as silly, pretentious, and unnatural, . . . Steinbeck's treatment of American moral decline as superficial, and its setting as unrealized" (Kaspareck 31). As Joseph Fontenrose pithily put it, "Ethan Hawley is improbable, and so is his story" (137). What were Saul Bellow, Edward Weeks, and Lewis Gannett thinking when they proclaimed on the dust jacket that *The Winter of Our Discontent* is "the finest thing Steinbeck has written since *The Grapes of Wrath*" and "one of his best"?

What they were thinking, if I may be so bold, is the truth about this marvelous book. *Time* does not allow for a careful review of the back-peddling of critics concerning *Winter*; as with Peter Lisca, most have recovered from their first impressions and have gone on to laud the novel's rich allusions to the Bible, Jungian psychology, Arthurian legend, and American history; its extraordinary narrative risk-taking; its prescience for the times. I will quote but one, Reloy Garcia, because his reassessment is so brutally honest:

> Several years ago I had the pleasure of writing an essay on . . . *The Winter of Our Discontent* for inclusion in *A Study Guide to Steinbeck: A Handbook to His Major Works*. . . . In preparation for this brief introduction [to a *Study Guide (Part II)*] I re-read that book, in the process immodestly reviewing my own theme. Reality is a harsh mistress, and I would write that essay differently today. . . . The book I then so impetuously criticized as somewhat thin, now strikes me as a deeply penetrating study of the American condition. I did not realize, at the time, that we had a condition. . . . [Steinbeck's] work thus rewards a returning reader, is seemingly amplified by our own enriched experience. (4)

In this essay I would like to offer some reasons why Bellow, Weeks, and Gannett were dead on the mark in 1961 and why Steinbeck scholarship since has had to play catch up.

With these authors I would contend that, given its multi-layered complexity, intriguing artistry, and clear moral purpose, *The Winter of Our Discontent* ranks in the upper echelon of Steinbeck's fiction, alongside *Of Mice and Men, Cannery Row, East of Eden*, and, of course, *The Grapes of Wrath*. I also believe that Steinbeck, in the guise of his alter-ego Ethan Hawley, is in effect "pulling a frog" face at all those critics who thought him artistically dead at the ripe old age of fifty-nine, that though their myopic reviews of the novel left him depressed, it is the author who has the last laugh today (3). Put simply, *The Winter of Our Discontent* is one of his finest literary creations.

As shown by examinations of the novel from such scholars as Michael Meyer, Lorelie Cederstrom, Carol Ann Kasparek, and Barbara Heavilin,[1] there are many means by which to support such a claim. However, the focus here will be on the contemporary nature of the novel, both in terms of the artistic process by which it was created and the immediate social context to which it is responding. Steinbeck epigraphically warns that those "seeking to identify the fictional people and places here described would do better to inspect their own communities and search their own hearts, for this book is about a large part of America today." No other novel, with the possible exception of *The Grapes of Wrath*, is so connected to the sense of place beyond its covers. *Winter*, Steinbeck's most "contemporary" novel, is inextricably bound to the national scandals of the 1950's and the author's increasing concerns over the moral direction and integrity of the nation.

Steinbeck was always ahead of his time. He was environmentally conscious before the Sierra Club opened its first office; he was encouraging new forms of literature, such as the "play-novelette," when most were content to mimic Hemingway. The same is true of the artistic process by which *The Winter of Our Discontent* was created—at an age when many authors are compiling their memoirs, Steinbeck engaged in a writing process that personified the idea of "contemporariness." Putting aside his work on the Arthurian Cycle (which would later be posthumously published as *The Acts of King Arthur and His Noble Knights*), the writer began a novel exploring the same themes of national and individual corruption. In order to tie *Winter's* theme of the loss of moral integrity to its immediate context, John Steinbeck wrote the novel during the same period of time as its setting—from Good Friday to July 4—a strikingly original thing to do and, as the writer admits, something "I . . . [had] never done . . . before"[2] (*Life in Letters* 633). Moreover, Steinbeck unabashedly makes its location the area in which he was then living, with New Baytown a thinly veiled Sag Harbor. The setting of *The Winter of Our Discontent* could not be more immediate if it had been a transcript from the downtown diner where Steinbeck regularly breakfasted; for all we know, some of it was.

The writer's artistry is also contemporary in its deliberate use of postmodern techniques—primarily with fragmented, shifting narrative voice—that correspond with the cutting edge fiction of the time. Most early critics condemned such experimentation; Warren French, in "Steinbeck's Winter Tale," argued that the mixed use of first- and third-person narration resulted in "the destruction of any consistent identification between Hawley and the reader" (74), while *The New Republic* complained of "the absence of a controlling point of view" in this clear literary "failure" (Crisler, McElrath, and Shillinglaw). However, later scholars disagree. John Ditsky notes that *Winter* is "a novel about mirrors," with the "double narrational voice" bringing "a sort of objectivity in [Ethan's] . . . moral vision of himself" (25). Further, after the third person perspective of the first two chapters of Part One and Two, the primary narration of first person takes over, thus allowing the juxtaposition of the outer Ethan (what everyone sees) with what Bob DeMott calls "Hawley's inner life" (94). Such inside/outside perspectives of Ethan Hawley allow the creation of what is perhaps

Steinbeck's richest character—an American "Everyman" as well as a
nobody grocery clerk in a "wop store" (4), a symbol of integrity to
Marullo co-existing as a fragmented and fallen Lancelot to Danny and
his daughter Ellen.

What these shifts in narrative voice reveal is startling—and disturbing if the reader is expecting the removed third person of *Of Mice and
Men* or the participatory narrator/character of *East of Eden*. Except
for a few short stories such as "Breakfast" or "Johnny Bear," in no
other work does John Steinbeck employ first person narration as the
primary vehicle of story telling (Simmonds 205). Yet in telling the
story primarily from a fragmented first-person perspective, the author
shows the corruption of a man's character in a way impossible to ren-
der in real life, for not only do we have access to Ethan's words and actions, we know his dreams, his memories, his searing moral conflicts,
his deepest moral ponderings. This experimentation also provides
"an additional perspective on our initial perception not only of Ethan
but also [on] the other characters" (Simmonds 206). Clearly what
was initially perceived as a lack of narrative control by early reviewers
actually had an artistic purpose; after a lifetime of experimentation,
the Nobel Prize author must at last be credited with knowing what he
was doing as a writer.

Such is forcefully argued by Carolyn Hagen, who states that in
The Winter of Our Discontent Hawley's "point of view is intentionally ambiguous"—jumping from cynical sermons to can goods and
nightmare visions of Danny to internal conversations with Captain
Hawley and distancing banter with Mary—all in an attempt to reflect
"Hawley's alienated struggle" within himself as well as "humanity's
fragmented feelings of anxiety and fear . . . within an unpredictable
world" (6). It is this cacophony of voices—both within and without,
past and present—which leads to the initial confusion of readers who
have yet to realize that they are following not "what is" (the non-
teleological goal of Steinbeck's early fiction[3]) but "what is inside,"
for *Winter*, more so than any other Steinbeck work, is an interior
novel—an exploration and revelation of the thought processes of a
good man who chooses evil. Hence,

> *The Winter of Our Discontent* . . . is ambiguous not because [Hawley's] . . .
> point of view is confusing, but because it is a reflection of an individual's
> state of mind. The forces and values that shape one's state of mind can
> only be comprehended by the individual him/herself. By focusing on
> Hawley's dialogue, Steinbeck takes a postmodern look at the eclectic

mind of an individual and the discourse which frames its voice. If the voice of the novel is misunderstood, Hawley's discourse is ignored and the novel becomes disorganized. Yet if the voice is appreciated, the reader can find the sources which frame his/her own struggle through Hawley's fragmented language. (Hagen 10)

This fragmented depiction of the "disintegration of a man" (258) would be impossible without the writer's deliberate postmodern experimentation with narrative voice in this, his last novel. Contrary to those contemporaries who claimed otherwise, John Steinbeck remained artistically vibrant and innovative to the end.

Just as compelling, however, are the contemporary ties of *The Winter of Our Discontent* to the immediate social scandals of the late 1950s. Clearly *Winter* is an exploration of the condition that Reloy Garcia initially failed to notice and to which many Americans still remain oblivious. Steinbeck most fully describes this condition in an intimate letter to the head of the United Nations, Dag Hammarskjold, in 1959:

I arrived at home for the culmination of the TV scandal. Except as a sad and dusty episode, I am not deeply moved by the little earnest, cheating people involved, except insofar as they are symptoms of a general immorality which pervades every level of our national life and perhaps the life of the whole world. It is very hard to raise boys to love and respect virtue and learning when the tools of success are chicanery, treachery, self-interest, laziness and cynicism or when charity is deductible, the courts venal, the highest public official placid, vain, slothful and illiterate. (*Life in Letters* 612)

The specific incident of "general immorality" to which Steinbeck refers is, of course, the national scandal involving Charles Van Doren on the quiz show *Twenty-One*. A detailed exploration of *Winter* with this incident (as portrayed in the play *Night and Her Stars* and film *Quiz Show*) is given in Robert and Katharine Morsberger's fascinating essay, "Falling Stars," in volume one of the *Steinbeck Yearbook*.[4] But to summarize, Van Doren, the son of Columbia professor and Pulitzer prize-winning poet Mark Van Doren, agreed to accept answers in advance and become the show's reigning champion in order (as he rationalized) to encourage learning across the nation. A charming, handsome young elite, Van Doren indeed becomes an American celebrity and role model, encouraging "by example . . . scholarship, literature, and intellectuality" (Morsberger and Morsberger 55). He eventually earns a sum of $129,000 on *Twenty-One*, graces the cover of *Time* magazine, and accepts a paid position as a cultural correspondent on the *Today Show*, all while continuing to teach at Columbia (Morsberger and Morsberger 55–56). For an entire nation, Charles Van Doren becomes a symbol of all that is right with America.

Then in 1958 the bottom fell out. After the discovery of fraud on the period's most popular program, *Dotto*, other quiz shows receive heightened scrutiny. Herbert Stempel, the chubby World War II veteran with bad teeth and an IQ of 170 who had been replaced by Van Doren, eventually comes forward with charges that the show was rigged. Then James Snodgrass, another contestant, turns over three sealed, registered letters mailed to himself which contained the questions and answers to a future *Twenty-One* program. Finally, a congressional subcommittee brings Charles Van Doren in to testify concerning the show. Van Doren, having already lied about his innocence and the show's fairness, appears before the committee on November 2, 1959, and makes a complete and public confession concerning his deception. He and eighteen others are "arrested, convicted of perjury, and given suspended sentences" (Morsberger and Morsberger 57). And his life is never the same.

This national episode with Van Doren echoes throughout *The Winter of Our Discontent*. Like Charles Van Doren, Ethan Hawley is of aristocratic heritage, his descendants springing from the Pilgrims, patriots, and shipping captains of early American history and wielding great wealth and influence until his father lost the family fortune. Like Van Doren, Ethan is highly educated and a gentleman (albeit wearing a clerk's apron) with high moral ideals that his wife Mary derides as "old-fashioned fancy-pants ideas" (34). And like Charles Van Doren, Ethan succumbs to pressures both internal and external to shed his moral scruples in order to expand his influence. In the movie the barrage of rationalizations aimed at Van Doren is nearly overwhelming—in machine gun fashion television executives Dan Enright and Albert Freedman explain how receiving the questions ahead of time is not cheating, how he will be a role model for children around the nation, how it's just entertainment. Even though Charles initially rejects their arguments, the slick and focused sophistry eventually carries the day when he chooses, on live television, to answer a question he was previously asked on the Civil War. From this point on Charles's moral descent is rapid.

In much the same way, Ethan Hawley is persuaded to forsake his principles in order to be a success. Echoing Van Doren's obvious desire to please his own father, Ethan feels an intense shame as a man, provider, and Hawley for being nothing more than "a goddam cat . . . catching Marullo's mice" (4). His rationalizations for turning his boss over to immigration, robbing Mr. Baker's bank, and facilitating Danny Taylor's drinking himself to death are, however, much more ruthless. With the first person narrative allowing direct access to his moral and psychological fragmentation, we see the thought processes of Ethan at work: his analogy of business to war, where you're a hero for killing (101); his use of natural selection and survival of the fittest to justify murder, for in the end "the eaters [are no] more immoral than the eaten" (46); his decision to view moral principles and behavior with playful new eyes, as a game to be played until the "procedure and equipment and timing were as near perfect as possible" (214); and his underlying shift to a belief that morality is a relative concept—as Ethan puts it, "If the laws of thinking are the laws of things, then morals are relative too, and manners and sin—that's relative too in a relative universe. Has to be. No getting away from it" (56–57). Like Van Doren, Ethan Hawley rationalizes his way to the destruction of what matters most: his own sense of self-respect. And like Van Doren, Ethan suffers a loss of moral integrity, which is ultimately a personal virtue, a struggle of the lonely individual with his or her conscience amid intense pressures for self gain. As both Van Doren and Hawley painfully learn, self-respect is impossible without adherence to your innermost values and beliefs.

Yet in a further twist, in his devastation at his own son's plagiarized "I Love America" essay, Ethan Hawley also represents the principled father, Mark Van Doren. Again, the contemporary ties of the quiz show scandal to the novel are unmistakable; in discussing the plagiarism with the public relations executive from NBC (which is just coincidentally the same network for *Twenty-One*) the "well-tailored man" from "Dunscombe, Brock and Schwin" gushes, "Thank Christ we caught it in time—after all the quiz troubles and Van Doren and all" (270-71). Earlier in the novel Ethan slips and calls his designing son "Charles," as in Charles Van Doren (Morsberger and Morsberger 63-64), to which the petulant teenager replies, "How do you mean, Charles?" (72). Ethan's own reaction to Allen's callous dishonesty mirrors that of the senior Van Doren, who in a dramatic climax of the film exclaims to his son, "Your name is mine!" It is at this moment—when the ethical becomes the personal—that Charlie finally accepts responsibility for what he has done and decides to testify before the subcommittee. However, in Hawley's case there is no moral foundation to allow him to judge his son for betraying his own moral standards; Ethan stands self-condemned with Allen's "Who cares? Everybody does it. . . . I bet you took some in your time, because they all do" (273).

Just as the contemporariness of *The Winter of Our Discontent* cannot be appreciated apart from its artistry and social context, so does the book's immediacy continue with the current concern over our nation's future. If Ethan Hawley felt pressure, within and without, to conform to the corrupt moral standards of his own time, such pressures have only increased since the time of the novel's writing. As one ethical philosopher contends:

> The very stress on individualism, on competition, on achieving material success which so marks our society [today] also generates intense pressures to cut corners. To win an election, to increase one's income, to outsell competitors—such motives impel many to participate in forms of duplicity they might otherwise resist. The more widespread they judge these practices to be, the stronger will be the pressures to join, even compete, in deviousness. (Bok 244)

Whether it be a scandal in Olympic judging or a cover-up in the highest offices of the land, Steinbeck's last novel continues to resonate with modern readers struggling to find reasons for resisting their own Joey Morphys and Mr. Bakers. The sense of moral urgency rendered in *Winter* shifts easily into the twenty-first century.

The Winter of Our Discontent also offers light upon what some describe as one of America's darkest hours. Since the terrorist attacks on the World Trade Center on September 11, 2001, our country has experienced an outpouring of patriotic zeal not seen since the attack on Pearl Harbor and opening of World War II—flags once thought passé are now sported on homes from Maine to California, the national anthem has become the feature attraction at athletic events, and writing contests across the country now focus on topics such as "patriotism," "freedom," "democracy," and our "American ideals."[5] Again, Steinbeck's *Winter* rings with a contemporary note, even in Allen Hawley's plagiarized "I Love America" essay, which ends with the stirring words: "Let us look to our country, elevate ourselves to the dignity of pure and disinterested patriots, and save our country from all impending dangers. What are we—what is any man—worth who is not ready and willing to sacrifice himself for his country?" (271).

In the aftermath of the terrorist attack of September 11, we have seen men and women who indeed were "willing to sacrifice" themselves for their country. The final redemptive act at the novel's end, when Ethan rejects suicide and struggles out of the sea to return the family talisman to its new owner, his daughter Ellen, has been played out again in the sacrifice of firefighters, police, rescue workers, military personnel, and even civilians aboard a plane over Pennsylvania, all of whom have given their lives—some figuratively, some literally—in reaffirming what is best about America.[6] However (and here's the rub), we must also remember that this essay calling us to "the dignity of . . . disinterested" patriotism was, ironically, submitted in the novel by a teenager morally disconnected from its application in his own life; for Allen Hawley, Ethan's future namesake, such "patriotic jazz" is for "squares" and merely a means to the fortune and fame he desires (71, 261). If *The Winter of Our Discontent* indeed captures a contemporary state of mind as a book "about a large part of America," we might do well to question our own professions of patriotism, commitments to causes, and honesty in dealing with those around us.

I have considered such questions personally in preparing this essay. In particular, on a cold January morning I was coaxed awake at 5:00 a.m. by my own Charles, a precocious eight-month-old who refused to go back to sleep. I went downstairs with this blue-eyed, glowing little fellow, found a comfortable spot on our futon, and put on Redford's *Quiz Show*. I think we often make moral excuses in the dark that we would shrink from in the light; in the early morning hours this movie's images of corruption and evil were more disturbing that I had ever remembered. Watching another Charles in a game show booth struggle with his conscience brought to my mind several sets of fathers and sons: Van Doran and his father Mark; Steinbeck and his sons Thom and Johnny; Ethan Hawley and a cynical, streetwise Allen; and me with my own boy slumbering on my chest. As I looked down at my son's tousled hair and complete inner peace, I thought of the film's morning scene with Van Doren and his dad, and Charlie's aching desire, after his duplicity, for those morally simple days of coming home to a glass of ice-cold milk and chocolate cake. As with all these fathers, I wondered if my own son would be true to his family name, honor the promptings of his conscience, and understand that there *are* moments of moral clarity—despite all the shades of gray—when we do know what is the right thing to do.

The Winter of Our Discontent, one of Steinbeck's finest and most daring novels, speaks directly to these core issues. It not only explores the depths of individual and societal corruption with its vanguard use of setting and postmodern narrative technique, it offers insight into the means for our redemption. *Winter*—like *Hamlet,* the Bible, and Dante's *Inferno*—is a work whose theme is for the ages. A contemporary audience would be wise to listen lest its final words prove true and another light goes out.

NOTES

1. Michael Meyer states in "Steinbeck's *The Winter of Our Discontent* (1961)" (in *A New Study Guide to Steinbeck's Major Works,* edited by Tetsumaro Hayashi) that the critical tide has turned concerning *Winter,* with scholars now finding in this "interweaving of biblical, historical, and literary texts" a moral insight and "complexity" which was initially overlooked (268). Such a sea change in critical thought has led to the first volume of the *Steinbeck Yearbook,* edited by Barbara Heavilin, to be entirely devoted to the novel.

2. As Roy Simmonds notes in *A Biographical and Critical Introduction of John Steinbeck,* the exact time period of the composition of the novel's first draft was from March 1 to the middle of July 1960 (200).

3. The best discussion of Steinbeck's (and Edward Rickett's) non-teleological approach to life is found in *The Log from the Sea of Cortez,* chapter 14, "Easter Sunday." Here the author points out the error in examining the "why" of something (teleology) without fully appreciating and understanding "what is." By the time of *The Winter of Our Discontent,* a mature Steinbeck seems to have satisfied himself with "what is" the moral state of the country and has now moved on to explore the "why."

4. In yet another instance of how contemporary *Winter* remains, the Morsbergers conclude their essay by observing that in the year 2000 quiz and game "shows are back and all the rage, and Americans trust one another now even less than when Steinbeck bemoaned the loss of trust as a . . . symptom and symbol of national malaise" (71).

5. A September 24, 2001, *Newsweek* article entitled "We Shall Overcome" reported that the American flag now flew "across America and the world," from the windows of "trucks barreling down Los Angeles freeways" to the gates of Buckingham Palace (18).

6. Another *Newsweek* article from December 3 attempts to piece together the heroic actions aboard Flight 93, which finally crashed near the town of

Shanksville, Pennsylvania. In an eerie echo of *Winter's* plagiarized essay, its epigraph reads, in part, "But a band of patriots came together to defy death and save a symbol of freedom" (54).

WORKS CITED

Bok, Sissela. *Lying: Moral Choice in Public and Private Life.* New York: Vintage, 1989.

Crisler, Jesse S., Joseph R. McElrath Jr., and Susan Shillinglaw. *John Steinbeck: The Contemporary Reviews.* Cambridge: Cambridge UP, 1996.

DeMott, Robert. "The Interior Distances of John Steinbeck." *Steinbeck Quarterly* 12 (1979): 86–99.

Ditsky, John. "The Devil Quotes Scripture: Biblical Misattribution and *The Winter of Our Discontent.*" *San Jose Studies* 15.2 (1989): 19–28.

Fontenrose, Joseph. *John Steinbeck: An Introduction and Interpretation.* New York: Barnes and Noble, 1963.

French, Warren. "Steinbeck's Winter Tale." *Modern Fiction Studies* 11 (1965): 66–74.

Garcia, Reloy. Introduction. *A Study Guide to Steinbeck (Part II).* Ed. Tetsumaro Hayashi. Metuchen, NJ: Scarecrow, 1979. 4–5.

Hagen, Carolyn A. "John Steinbeck's *The Winter of Our Discontent:* Post-modern Discourse or Structural Ambiguity?" Address. John Steinbeck's Americas: A Centennial Conference. Hempstead, NY. 23 Mar. 2002.

Kasparek, Carol Ann. *Ethan's Quest Within: A Mythic Interpretation of John Steinbeck's* The Winter of Our Discontent. Diss. Ball State U, 1983. Ann Arbor: UMI, 1983 8401282.

Lisca, Peter. "Steinbeck's Image of Man and His Decline as a Writer." *Modern Fiction Studies* 11 (1965): 3–10.

Morsberger, Robert E., and Katharine M. Morsberger. "Falling Stars: The Quiz Show Scandal in Steinbeck's *The Winter of Our Discontent,* Richard Greenberg's *Night and Her Stars,* and Robert Redford's *Quiz Show.*" *Steinbeck Yearbook.* Vol. 1. Ed. Barbara A. Heavilin. Lewiston, NY: Mellen, 2000. 47–76.

Quiz Show. Screenplay by Richard N. Goodwin and Paul Attanasio. Dir. Robert Redford. Prod. Richard Dreyfuss, Richard N. Goodwin, Michael Jacobs, and Judith James. Perf. Ralph Fiennes, Rob Morrow, John Turturro, and Paul Schofield. Videocassette. Hollywood Pictures/Buena Vista, 1994.

Simmonds, Roy. *A Biographical and Critical Introduction of John Steinbeck.* Lewiston, NY: Mellen, 2000.

Steinbeck, Elaine, and Robert Wallsten, eds. *Steinbeck: A Life in Letters.* New York: Viking, 1975.

Steinbeck, John. *The Winter of Our Discontent.* New York: Penguin, 1996.

4

"Only through Imitation Do We Develop towards Originality"

Reflections of Addison's *Spectator* in Steinbeck's *Travels with Charley*

Barbara A. Heavilin
Taylor University

> Only through imitation do we develop towards originality.
>
> —Steinbeck in *Travels with Charley in Search of America*

> Among the books I had brought along, I saw a well-remembered cover and brought it out to the sunlight—a golden hand holding at once a serpent and a mirror with wings, and below in scriptlike letters "The Spectator, Edited by Henry Morley."
>
> —John Steinbeck in *Travels with Charley in Search of America*

> Very early I conceived a love for Joseph Addison which I have never lost. He plays the instrument of language as Casals plays a cello. I do not know whether he influenced my prose style, but I could hope he did.
>
> —John Steinbeck in *Travels with Charley in Search of America*

John Steinbeck's fascination with British writers has been well documented, particularly his lifelong love of the fourteenth-century Sir Thomas Malory's *Le Morte D'Arthur: Book of King Arthur and of His Noble Knights of the Round Table*. His acknowledged indebtedness to British writers of the eighteenth-century, however, has not been as

carefully considered, with the exception of my study of Henry Fielding's influence on *East of Eden,* which is based on Steinbeck's letter to
Pascal Covici baring his intention to write a book in which the "pace
. . . is more like Fielding than Hemingway" (*Journal of a Novel: the East
of Eden Letters* 29). He acknowledges similar ties to the eighteenth century in *Travels with Charley.* Early in his journey with his wife's French
poodle, Charley, he finds among the books he "had brought along . . .
a well-remembered cover and brought it out to the sunlight—a golden
hand holding at once a serpent and a mirror with wings, and below in
scriptlike letters 'The Spectator, Edited by Henry Morley.'" Seeing the
volume brings back childhood memories:

> I seem to have had a fortunate childhood for a writer. My grandfather,
> Sam'l Hamilton, loved good writing, and he knew it too. . . . Thus it was
> that in Salinas, in the great dark walnut bookcase with the glass doors,
> there were strange and wonderful things to be found. . . . Very early I
> conceived a love for Joseph Addison, which I have never lost. He plays
> the instrument of language as Casals plays a cello. I do not know whether
> he influenced my prose style, but I could hope he did. In the White
> Mountains in 1960, sitting in the sun, I opened the well-remembered
> first volume, printed in 1883." (37–38)

Although Steinbeck does not make quite so explicit his intention to
emulate Joseph Addison as he does to adopt Fielding's slow-paced
style, he associates himself closely with Addison, devoting some six
pages to him—even an imitation of his eighteenth-century style,
choice of topic, and reader consideration in *The Spectator:*

> I opened the well-remembered first volume, printed in 1883. I turned to
> Number 1 of The Spectator—Thursday, March 1, 1711. . . . I remember
> so well loving Addison's use of capital letters for nouns. He writes under
> this date: "I have observed that a Reader seldom peruses a Book with
> Pleasure 'till he knows whether the Writer of it be a black or fair Man,
> of a mild or cholerick Disposition, married, or a Batchelor, with other
> Particulars of the like Nature, that conduce very much to the right Un-
> derstanding of an Author. To gratify this Curiosity, which is so natural to
> a Reader, I design this Paper and my next as Prefatory Discourses to my
> following Writings and shall give some Account in them of the several
> persons that are engaged in this Work. As the chief trouble of Compil-
> ing, Digesting and Correcting will fall to my Share, I must do myself the
> Justice to open the Work with my own History." (38–39)

Following Addison's precedent, Steinbeck writes, "Sunday, January 29, 1961. Yes, Joseph Addison I hear and I will obey within Reason, for it appears that Curiosity you speak of has in no Way abated" (39). And, in Addison's style, he provides the reader a description of his appearance and attire, followed by a brief musing on the mind's capacity for doing two things at once as he is interrupted by Charley's amorous adventure with "a rather stout and bedizened Pomeranian of the female persuasion" (41).

Steinbeck's feeling of affinity for Addison goes beyond imitation and a desire for a style like that of this eighteenth-century writer, who "plays the instrument of language as Casals plays a cello" (37). Both writers view themselves as spectators, with Addison adopting the name, Mr. Spectator, as he goes about London and its environs, wittily and learnedly commenting on what he sees. Steinbeck similarly travels across America. Robert DeMaria Jr. refers to *The Spectator* as "a kind of extension and apotheosis of coffee-house chat," with both helping to "create the public sphere of private individuals" (664). Steinbeck's truck, Rocinante—in which he delights to entertain and converse with guests along the way—together with conversations (or sometimes comments on the lack thereof) in roadside restaurants provide a similar sense of a "public sphere of private individuals" in *Travels with Charley*.

Writing within this public sphere, both writers were naturally social thinkers and critics, commenting on and guiding readers' thoughts and tastes. The emblematic depiction on the cover of *The Spectator*—"a golden hand holding at once a serpent and a mirror with wings"—has significance not only for Addison's Mr. Spectator as he wanders about London observing and commenting on life as he sees it but also for Steinbeck's journey in search of America. These emblems may best be discussed first in their separate components. The *Dictionary of Symbolism* defines *gold* as "illuminating, sacred, . . . precious."[1] The *hand*, according to Aristotle, "is the 'tool of tools'" and may be associated with "strength, power and protection." Taken together, then, the golden hand represents *The Spectator*, suggesting that the efficacy of the written word illuminates and thus empowers its readers—knowledge is power.

This golden hand holds two objects, the first a *serpent*, which may represent evil, and the second "*a mirror with wings*." The mirror—the most common emblem employed in eighteenth-century satire—is that object which the satirist held before society in the hope that human beings might see themselves with all of their foibles and wickedness and, it was hoped, reform or, in its more Juvenalian manifestations, to despair and abandon hope. Addison, like Steinbeck, however, always believes in the possibility of reform, symbolized by the mirror's wings. The *Dictionary of Symbolism* suggests that "winged creatures are often messengers of the gods, and they are a symbol of freedom and spirituality." The winged mirror, then, may be taken as a symbol of illumination and of hope.

Taking the separate components together, the emblem of the "golden hand holding at once a serpent and a mirror with wings" reveals *The Spectator*'s commitment to its society—a commitment Steinbeck shares. As thinkers, Mr. Spectator comments on the London scene, sharing ideas along the way; and John Steinbeck, on an American vista, likewise sharing viewpoints on the world at large. As critics, both hope to correct human foibles by exposing them. Both seek first to inform themselves—Addison in order to report truly and Steinbeck in order to gain a fresh, accurate view of the country he loves.

The similarities between *The Spectator* and *Travels with Charley*, however, go beyond those of authorial intention. Steinbeck's affectionate musings on Addison, after all, lead him to hope that his own prose style had been influenced by this eighteenth-century writer. And there are readily observable similarities between the two writers: both are thinkers, social commentators, and critics. They share significant commonalities: (1) their observations of the workings of their own mind across time as a writing topic, (2) their use of fictional dialogue[2] in their portrayal of events and people, and (3) their use of the overlying generalization—an epigrammatic moral observation on the nature of people and things.

OBSERVATIONS OF THE WORKINGS OF THE MIND

William H. Youngren's study in "Addison and the Birth of Eighteenth-Century Aesthetics" centers around concerns with the observation of the workings of the mind across time, maintaining that from the beginnings of *The Spectator*,

> time, and especially the ways in which the mind works through time, are primary concerns of the persona Addison and Steele are creating. Mr.

Spectator is, in fact, as much a spectator of mental activity (his own and other people's) as of the external world of London and the Club. "The working of my own Mind," Steele has him say (No. 4), "is the general Entertainment of my Life." (1:21) (275)

The "working" of the mind, then, occurs in a blank space that may be filled over time—here following the lead of the philosopher Locke's metaphor of the mind as a *tabula rasa* (white sheet) and as a room to be furnished.[3]

Determining to learn all he possibly can in the search for his country, like Addison, Steinbeck observes how his own mind will work during his journey: "I had to be peripatetic eyes and ears, a kind of moving gelatin plate" (6). Across time and space, imprints and impressions would be formed on the "moving gelatin plate" of his mind. Like Addison, too, he views the mind as a space to be filled, contemplating on the nature of thinking. In one of the book's fictional dialogues, for instance, when Steinbeck stops at a farm to buy fresh eggs, the farmer permits him to park Rocinante by a stream for the night. Hospitably inviting the farmer into his truck-turned-coffeehouse, Steinbeck invites him in for coffee with "a good dollop of twenty-one-year-old applejack." Over this congenial beverage, they enter into a conversation on Krushchev, the U.N., the election, and speculations on ways of knowing and thinking. The farmer remembers his grandfather's assured view of the world: "'Nobody knows. What good's an opinion if you don't know? My grandfather knew the number of whiskers in the Almighty's beard. I don't even know what happened yesterday, let alone tomorrow. . . . We've got nothing to go on—got no way to think about things'" (32). The conversation leads to musings on time and thought:

> Maybe he had put his finger on it. Humans had perhaps a million years to get used to fire as a thing and as an idea. Between the time a man got his finger burned on a lightning-struck tree until another man carried some inside a cave and found it kept him warm, maybe a hundred thousand years, and from there to the blast furnaces of Detroit—how long?
>
> And now a force was in hand how much more strong, and we hadn't had time to develop the means to think, for man has to have feelings and then words before he can come close to thought and, in the past, at least, that has taken a long time. (32–33)

The "force" to which Steinbeck refers is undoubtedly the threat of atomic warfare some feared would follow the drawn-out cold war between Russia and the United States. Faced with the possibility of annihilation such as had been witnessed in the unspeakable horror of the attack on the cities of Hiroshima and Nagasaki, humanity simply did not have the capacity to comprehend its world.

In addition to contemplating about how human beings think, Steinbeck spends much time on this journey considering whether or not he is learning anything—whether he is filling that blank space of his mind on this peripatetic journey, designed to rediscover his country and its people and to gain a feeling of what they are like. Parking Rocinante "well away from the road and from any traffic," he discusses the matter with Charley: "I did not put aside my sloth for the sake of a few amusing anecdotes. I came with the wish to learn what America is like. And I wasn't sure I was learning anything" (140). He muses on this question all across the country to California and then back across to Abingdon, Virginia. Steinbeck fears at one point that he has passed his "limit of taking it in," that he is now experiencing "the stuffed and helpless inability to see more" (221). He discusses the matter with Charley, who suggests, "'Let's take a stroll up the hill. . . . Maybe you've started again'" (224). Steinbeck recognizes the truth in the statement; seeing the night "prickled with fiery dots," he observes, "My light brought an answering flash up the steep rocky bank. I climbed up, slipping and floundering, lost the echoed light and found it again, a good little new-split stone with mica in it—not a fortune but a good thing to have. I put it in my pocket and we went to bed" (224). He has started once more to furnish the room of his mind, as he had hoped, to see again.

In Abingdon, Virginia, the longing for home takes precedence over his desire to see and to learn. From that point on, Steinbeck simply ticks off the miles, like Odysseus, driven by the vision of home awaiting him. His mind now is passive as he is carried along by New York's "river of traffic" (276). The "gelatin plate" of his mind is as full as it is going to get for now, the "room of his mind furnished with as many musings and observations as it will hold for the time being. At the end of the journey, his "body was in a nerveless, tireless vacuum" (276).

Steinbeck shares with Addison a further concern with the nature of seeing, thinking, and knowing—the realm of the imagination in its response to the awes of nature and the concepts of sensibility and the sublime. Although these concepts are often connected with the Romantics, Addison is their precursor, and Steinbeck reflects the same concern with exalted, perhaps even inspired, thought.

Youngren observes that Addison labors "to express his deepening sense of the complexity of the mind's action, as it responds through time to the greatness, beauty, and novelty found in the natural world"—qualities that the writer finally calls the "'Pleasures of the imagination, which arise from the actual View and Survey of outward Objects" (3:550) (280).

Steinbeck describes such "Pleasures of the imagination" and the experience of the sublime when he visits Wisconsin on "a fair autumn day, . . . crisp and clean" (125):

> I saw it for the first time in early October, the air was rich with butter-colored sunlight, not fuzzy but crisp and clear so that every frost-gay tree was set off, the rising hills were not compounded, but alone and separate. There was a penetration of the light into solid substance so that I seemed to see into things, deep in, and I've seen that kind of light elsewhere only in Greece. . . . It was a magic day. The land dripped with richness, the fat cows and pigs gleaming against the green, and, in the smaller holdings, corn standing in little tents as corn should, and pumpkins all about. (126)

This experience of the sublime is again connected with light when Steinbeck enters the Bad Lands in North Dakota.

On initial impression, he describes the Bad Lands as "a place the Fallen Angels might have built as a spite to Heaven, dry and sharp, desolate and dangerous, and for me filled with foreboding" (154). As he hurries "to get away from the unearthly landscape" before nightfall, the late afternoon light changes everything:

> As the sun angled, the buttes and coulees, the cliffs and sculptured hills and ravines lost their burned and dreadful look and glowed with yellow and rich browns and a hundred variations of red and silver gray, all picked out by streaks of coal black. It was so beautiful that I stopped near a thicket of dwarfed and wind-warped cedars and junipers, and once stopped I was caught, trapped in color and dazzled by the clarity of the light. . . . And the night, far from being frightful, was lovely beyond thought, for the stars were close, and although there was no moon the starlight made a silver glow in the sky. . . . In the night the Bad Lands had become Good Lands. (156–57)

Just as Addison labors "to express his deepening sense of the complexity of the mind's action, as it responds through time to the greatness, beauty, and novelty found in the natural world," so Steinbeck finds mere words inadequate for the scene he beholds. "Lovely beyond thought"—Steinbeck thus captures elegantly the nature of the sublime. "Caught," "trapped" by awe in the presence of great beauty, he reverses his initial impression—bathed in light, the Bad Lands have become Good Lands.

Contemplation on a topic is another means of thinking in *The Spectator*. In Addison's Thursday, July 3, 1712, discussion of the "Pleasures of the Imagination," topics are delineated in a contents page, such as, for example, *"The Perfection of our Sight above our other Senses," "Why the Necessary Cause of our being pleased with what is Great, New, or Beautiful, unknown,"* and *"How a whole Set of Ideas Hang together."*[3] Similarly, Steinbeck makes "some notes on a yellow paper on the nature and quality of being alone," titles them "Relationship Time to Aloneness," and absentmindedly wraps the notes around a bottle of ketchup, tying them with a rubber band. Finding them later, he comments that "when the quality of aloneness settles down," time ceases to have meaning as memories, present events, and forecasts are "all equally present" (137). Remembering his own experience with being alone "for two succeeding years . . . each winter for eight months at a stretch in the Sierra Nevada mountains on Lake Tahoe," he muses that he stopped whistling and conversing with his dogs as "subtleties of feeling began to disappear until finally I was on a pleasure-pain basis" (137). He concludes that it may be that "a man who has no one to say anything to has no words as he has no need for words" (138). Steinbeck seems to fill this need for the warmth of association and communication with fictional dialogue[4]—some of it of the canine variety as Charley takes on the role of converser.

USE OF FICTIONAL DIALOGUE

This use of fictional dialogue, too, Steinbeck shares with Addison. Charles A. Knight's "The *Spectator's* Moral Economy," to illustrate, cites *Spectator*, no. 11's depiction of an instance of the "tragic manifestation of misplaced mercantilism," a story that occurs in a conversation between the charming and learned Arietta and "a Common-Place Talker" on the relative constancy of women and men in affairs of love. Angered by the typically male position presented by this "Common-Place Talker," Arietta tells the story of Inkle and Yarico:

Inkle had been educated with "particular Care to instill into his Mind an early Love of Gain, by making him a perfect Master of Numbers, and consequently giving him a quick View of Loss and Advantage." The success of this education is grimly illustrated after Inkle's rescue by an Indian maid with whom he falls in love. He sells her and their unborn child into slavery because he begins "to weigh with himself how many Days Interest of his Mony he had lost during his Stay with Yarico. (171)

Just as Addison's story of Inkle and Yarico underscores the horrors of an obsession with gain at the expense of the most humane values—love of family and a child—so Steinbeck encapsulates the impact of racial discrimination in the South as portrayed in the withered and diminished spirit of an old African-American man whom Steinbeck gives a ride.

Before the encounter with this man, in New Orleans Steinbeck had just witnessed United States marshals escorting "the littlest Negro girl you ever saw," protecting marshals lining the walk on each side—a token integration of the public school. She was accompanied, too, by the crowd's obscene jeers and taunts. But this was not the "big show" for which the crowd waited:

The crowd was waiting for the white man who dared to bring his white child to school. And here he came along the guarded walk, a tall man dressed in light gray, leading his frightened child by the hand. . . . The muscles of his cheeks stood out from the clenched jaws, a man afraid who by his will held his fears in check as a great rider directs a panicked horse. (257)

Accompanying the scene is a cacophony of voices as one person after another shouts obscenities, "the words bestial and filthy and degenerate" and each followed by "howls and roars and whistles of applause (257–58).

Sickened, Steinbeck leaves the scene and later is compelled to stop to offer the old Black man a ride. The story captures the essence of the Black experience. Trudging "with heavy heels in the grass-grown verge beside the concrete road," the old Black man accepts a ride reluctantly,

as though helpless to resist. He wore the battered clothes of a field hand and an ancient broadcloth coat highly polished by age and wear. . . . He clasped his hands in his lap, knotted and lumpy as cherry twigs, and all of him seemed to shrink in the seat as though he sucked in his outline to make it smaller.

He never looked at me. I could not see that he looked at anything. But first he asked, "Dog bite, captain, sir?"

"No. He's friendly."

After a long silent while I asked, "How are things going with you?"

"Fine, just fine, captain, sir."

"How do you feel about what's going on?"

He didn't answer.

"I mean about the schools and the sit-ins."

"I don't know nothing about that, captain, sir."

"Work on a farm?"

"Crop a cotton lot, sir."

We went in silence for a stretch upriver. . . . After a time I said, more to myself than to him, "After all, why should you trust me? A question is a trap and an answer is your foot in it." I remembered a scene . . . and was moved to tell him about it, but I quickly abandoned the impulse because out of the corner of my eye I could see that he had drawn away and squeezed himself against the far side of the cab." (266–67)

The old man squirms restlessly and asks to get out because he lives nearby. In the rearview mirror Steinbeck watches him trudging away alongside the road—"He didn't live nearby at all, but walking was safer than riding with me." But in his mind's eye he still sees "the old man squeezed as far away from me as he could get, as though I carried the infection." Like Addison, Steinbeck captures one of the horrors of his time, with prejudice setting people against one another and the resulting "tension, a weight of savage fear, . . . building pressure like a boil, . . . the breath of fear . . . everywhere" (268).

OVERLYING MORAL GENERALIZATIONS

Overlying generalizations—those pithy epigrammatic statements that can stand alone to make a moral statement or a pithy observation—are part and parcel of the eighteenth-century's concern with the human condition. In the Thursday, May 3, 1711, edition of *The Spectator*, to illustrate, Addison opens with the statement that "most of the Trades, Professions, and Ways of Living among Mankind, take their Original either from the Love of Pleasure or the Fear of Want. The former, when it becomes too violent, degenerates into *Luxury*, and the latter into *Avarice*."

In the same issue, he offers similar generalizations: "Avarice and Luxury very often become one complicated Principle of Action, in those whose Hearts are wholly set upon Ease, Magnificence, and Pleasure" and "Avarice supplies *Luxury* in the room of *Plenty*, as *Luxury* prompts Avarice in the place of *Poverty*."

Steinbeck states his intention to generalize—or to arrive at larger truths—while he is preparing for his journey: "I determined to look again, to try to rediscover this monster land. Otherwise, in writing, I could not tell the small diagnostic truths which are the foundations of the larger truth" (6). And, like Addison, he sprinkles his writing with generalizations:

> There's a gentility on the road. A direct or personal question is out of bounds. But this is simple good manners anywhere in the world. (30)

> A sad soul can kill you quicker, far quicker, than a germ. (48)

> Only through imitation do we develop towards originality. (138)

> Every safe generality I gathered in my travels was canceled by another. In the night the Bad Lands had become Good Lands. I can't explain it. That's how it was. (157)

Contemplating America, Steinbeck engages in what he calls "this generality jazz," and under subheads he speculates about what he has discovered thus far. Of food, he states, "America . . . has put cleanliness first, at the expense of taste" (141). Of reading, he observes, "The big-city papers cast their shadows over large areas around them, the *New York Times* as far as the Great Lakes, the *Chicago Tribune* all the way here to North Dakota" (141–42). Then he trails off into queries, themselves implied generalizations: "If this people has so atrophied its taste buds as to find tasteless food not only acceptable but desirable, what of the emotional life of the nation?" (142)

"Only through imitation do we develop towards originality"—in brief, Steinbeck here captures the nature of his debt to Joseph Addison. Imitating him, sharing his roles as thinker, social critic, and observer of humankind, he emerges as Mr. American Spectator—a kindly relative of Addison's British Mr. Spectator and his keen observations of the London scene in his newspaper. Both writers are lovers of humanity, with faith in humankind's capacity for perfection. By means of a "golden hand"—representing the illumination and power of the written word—they both faithfully perform two essential functions of the social critic. First, by this enlightenment, they strive to hold back and thereby constrain the serpent of evil that threatens to undermine humanity. Second, they hold up the winged mirror of satire in order for society to see its faults and, it was hoped, correct them. Steinbeck's "originality," then, has deep roots in the eighteenth century and in Mr. Spectator, a writer whom he hoped to emulate.

NOTES

1. The *Dictionary of Symbolism* is located on an online site originally con-structed by Allison Protas at the University of Michigan.

2. See William H. Youngren's discussion of Lockean philosophy of the mind as a room to be "furnished" in "Addison and the Birth of Eighteenth-Century Aesthetics." *Modern Philology*, Vol. 79, No. 3, (Feb. 1982), 278. Locke's philosophy, he finds, goes beyond the concept of the *tabula rasa* to include that "which the busy and boundless fancy of man has painted on it with an almost endless variety":

> Books 2 and 3 of Locke's Essay are, in fact, filled with eloquent paeans to the power of the mind to shape and elaborate its experience. Far too much has been made of his statement that the understanding, in its reception of simple ideas, "is merely passive." Though this statement has seemed most threatening to post-Coleridgean literary historians, it is really quite sensible, indisputable (given Locke's terms), and innocent. (278)

3. References to *The Spectator* may be located at the following online site: Eighteenth-Century E-Texts—A, edited by Jack Lynch at http://andromeda. rutgers.edu/ ~jlynch/ 18th/ a.html. This project is a part of a larger collection of eighteenth-century e-texts.

4. I have purposefully chosen "fictional dialogue" rather than "creative nonfictional dialogue" (which Lee Gutkind defines as "high quality non-fiction prose [memoir, literary journalism, personal essay])" on the Cre-ative Nonfiction Foundation website (http://www.creativenonfiction.org/ cnf_foundation.html). The term seems an oxymoronic hybrid that I am not comfortable applying to *Travels with Charley*. Although they maintain the es-sence of the situation, the conversations are undoubtedly amended, extended, and polished. Besides, there is, after all, truth in fiction itself, even when a dog is one of the speakers.

WORKS CITED

DeMaria, Jr., Robert, ed. *British Literature 1640–1789: An Anthology.* Oxford: Blackwell Publishers, Inc., 1966.

Knight, Charles A. "The *Spectator's* Moral Economy." *Modern Philology,* Vol. 91, No. 2 (Nov. 1993), 161–79.

Steinbeck, John. *Journal of a Novel: The* East of Eden *Letters.* New York: The Viking Press, 1969.

Youngren, William H. "Addison and the Birth of Eighteenth-Century Aesthetics." *Modern Philology,* Vol. 79, No. 3 (Feb. 1982), 267–83.

5

Charley, America, and Malory

John Steinbeck's Later Ethics

John H. Timmerman
Calvin College

The setting on Nantucket Island during May 15–17, 1992, was a good one for a conference titled "Steinbeck and the Environment." Wind tossed across the green speckled sea; bits of sun fitfully twisted over the knob of rock. Whether in one of the meeting rooms or walking the narrow, arthritic streets, one had opportunities for informal talk with conferees. Furthermore, the book of essays that emerged from those discussions well represented the tenor and first rate scholarship of the conference.

A chance meeting there turned my thinking about Steinbeck in a new direction. I had for some time been paying close attention to ethical values in Steinbeck's fiction, a pursuit well explored in *East of Eden*, but less so in other works.[1] In this state of mind, I happened to meet Elaine Steinbeck in the hotel lobby one evening. She was obviously waiting to be met for dinner, but nonetheless our talk was leisurely and it turned to a work I had been rereading, *America and Americans*. I considered it an integral of Steinbeck's so-called moral trilogy, including *Travels with Charley* and *The Winter of Our Discontent*.

Elaine quickly agreed, adding that "John didn't like the way Viking produced the book. They saw it as a 'coffee table' book with pretty pictures."[2] I have the remark jotted down in my notes from the conference. What did it mean? A summation of his values in a production he disliked? To answer these questions, it is helpful to compare *America* with *Travels with Charley*, the first work of the so-called trilogy. An examination of the genesis of each work, the nature of the genre, and the summary argument of each is useful both to distinguish one from another and also to locate the accurate testimony of a moral vision. In each case, moreover, that testimony is colored by Steinbeck's ongoing work to translate and retell Malory's *Morte D' Arthur.*

Evidence indicates that *Travels with Charley*, or the mood precipitating the adventure, had long been on Steinbeck's mind. In fact, in *John Steinbeck, Writer*, Jackson Benson dates it to an October 6, 1954, letter to Elizabeth Otis:

> There is one thing I want to do. When I get home I want to sort of clear my mind and then do some work I have laid out but about the late spring I want to take a drive through the middle west and the south and listen to what the country is about now. I have been cut off for a very long time and I think it would be a valuable thing for me to do. New York is very far from the nation in some respects. And it isn't politics so much as the whole pattern. I have lost track of it I think. (767)

The urge accentuated as Steinbeck began to make plans. On May 25, 1960, he wrote Frank and Fatima Loesser that "in the fall—right after Labor Day—I'm going to learn about my own country. I've lost the flavor and taste and sound of it. It's been years since I've seen it. . . . It will be a kind of a rebirth" (Steinbeck and Wallsten 666).

The references to the senses in that letter are interesting. They signal his intention to immerse himself in his country, to experience it fully in order to find the real thing. By so doing, he would also be finding himself. The intimacy of Steinbeck's allusions is almost baptismal in its quality. Part of this self-discovery process was Steinbeck's method of pursuing bypaths as his instincts prompted him. This would by no means be a scripted tour.

What urged Steinbeck on led others to urge him to stay. The fact is that Steinbeck's health had been fragile for the last year, including a slight stroke. It isn't difficult to see Charley's bladder problems as something of an inverse objective correlative for Steinbeck. As he cares for the suffering dog, Steinbeck himself seems to acquire strength. But that lay in the future, and at the outset of the journey several people, including Elizabeth Otis, tried to dissuade him. Elaine was delighted when Steinbeck asked to borrow her dog (Charley was a gift to her), since then he would have someone to look after him.

Frequently categorized as "travel literature" or "road literature" in the vein of Kerouac or William Least Heat-Moon, *Charley* snuggles more neatly into a generic mode with which Steinbeck had been accustomed since his earliest writing-journalism. The attentive reader can find Steinbeck's journalistic aptitude and interest emerging already in his earliest work. For example, the subtitle to *Sea of Cortez* (1941) reads: *A Leisurely Journal of Travel and Research.* And before that, we have the 1938 series of seven articles Steinbeck wrote for the *San Francisco News* under the title, "The Harvest Gypsies."[3] Differences mark the three works to be sure. *Sea of Cortez* divides between keen description and an almost sermonic philosophical quality.[4] *Harvest Gypsies* suffers the constraints of reporting, which prompted Steinbeck to the novelistic task of *The Grapes of Wrath.* Even though distinguished by Steinbeck's inimitable style, journalistic pieces suffer the constraints of the intended venue. Nonetheless, Steinbeck's journalism may be characterized by three key elements.

Steinbeck's insatiable curiosity situates events in their immediate environment. This ruthless urge to sample the reality similarly fueled his fiction. Although some might want to bring finer distinctions, it could reasonably be argued that *East of Eden* is his only purely conceptual novel. A close contender for the category, of course, is *The Winter of Our Discontent,* fictional precursor to *Charley* and *America.* Perhaps because of his early tutelage under Ed Ricketts, furthermore, Steinbeck possessed the keen ability to penetrate past the appearance to the facts. Surely he was given at times to rather grandiose and general theories, such as his famed and flawed Group Man Theory. With maturity as a writer and a journalist, however, he penetrated analytically to the facts.

Nonetheless, even in his most objective journalism, he shared a point of view on the subject. Perhaps *Letters to Alicia* is one of the few exceptions simply because the Vietnam War appeared so baffling to him that he found real conclusions elusive. Yet, in the general pattern, Steinbeck readily extrapolated from fact to conclusion. Such also was his method in *Travels with Charley.*

These symbiotic characteristics of curiosity, analysis, and conclusion are not the norm in contemporary journalism. Especially the latter distinguishes Steinbeck, for precisely here the journalist donned the novelist's garments. Steinbeck is seldom explicit in the conclusions he derives from a novelistic event. Rather, he structures the work suggestively so that the reader is prompted to, but seldom shown, conclusions. It seems to me, although some have suggested such, that Steinbeck was never a didactic writer—at least until his later years. Whatever values he held were implicit, embedded in the narrative.

Fueled by disappointment with his perceived sense of the nation's course and with a growing sense of his own mortality, Steinbeck set out in Rocinante with Elaine's Charley. (The working title changed from "Operation America" to "Operation Windmills"; hence Rocinante.) In this sense, the key theme of the book is struck at the outset: "We find after years of struggle that we do not take a trip; a trip takes us" (4). Thus the metaphor of journey into himself. This places us at a perilous position within the twentieth-century tradition of journalism, and our understanding of it from the twenty-first. For what Steinbeck proposes here is not an objective summary of things seen and events recorded, but nothing less than a quest. The quest is not so much an adventure, which may begin or end at any time. A quest, and Steinbeck surely understood this from his previous several years of work on the Arthurian legends, is a pursuit of a lost or precious object. One doesn't know where it lies at the start; one will never know unless one starts. On the way certain obstacles must be overcome, and these surely arise in *Charley*, from his loneliness in Elaine's absence to his soul-numbing experience in New Orleans.

But above all, the precious object. It may indeed be an object, such as the Holy Grail. It may be a person desired or loved, such as Guinevere. Or, finally, it may be oneself, as in the case of Sir Lancelot. Translated to *Charley*, the precious object is America itself, the desired end in this case a renewed relationship with the land and with the person Steinbeck's own sense of self and well-being.

After the long journey, Steinbeck and Elaine left in February for Barbados. Steinbeck was not particularly comfortable there, preferring the familiar surroundings of Sag Harbor despite the winter cold. Nonetheless, the writing of *Charley* developed successfully and was released in early 1962. The success of Steinbeck's "dog book" astonished nearly everyone. Initial sales exploded, the book resided firmly on the *New York Times* best seller list for weeks, and subsidiary rights were sold to Book-of-the-Month Club, further expanding sales. While Steinbeck was pleased, Viking Press was ecstatic. Moreover, in October 1962, Steinbeck learned that he had won the Nobel Award for Literature. Viking, of course, wanted a repeat of *Charley* to work the publicity and fatten the coffers.

Thomas Guinzburg, then president of Viking Press, approached Steinbeck in August 1964, with a collection of photographs by many of the nation's foremost photographers—Ansel Adams, Alfred Eisenstaedt, and others. The photographs did indeed capture Steinbeck's imagination, and the idea of accompanying essays on the American spirit intrigued him. Although Guinzburg's original concept of the book was for Steinbeck to write an introduction and captions for the pictures, Steinbeck's mind quickly moved past that. This was to be a work in the fashion of de Tocqueville's *Democracy in America*. While the four-part sections of Charley show a man rediscovering his deep love for the land, America gave him an open forum to address a wide range of positive and negative values in that land.

These two facts—working from photographs and the open-ended forum to explore values—largely contribute to the dissonant and conflicting notes of the work. First, the photographic basis contravened Steinbeck's journalistic method of curiosity, fact, and conclusion. Photographs instead evoke different responses and emotions—beauty of the image, perhaps, but also a memory or attitude dredged to the foreground by the image. Second, instead of the personal point of view with *Charley*, Steinbeck had several convoluted points of view at hand. One was leftover portions of *Charley* that he thought he could include. Another was his deep bewilderment with the political chaos of the time, most prominently incarnated in the Vietnam War.[5]

Third was the essentially failed moral experiments of the Arthurian stories he had been translating. These tales always represented for him, as they certainly do in the original, a conflict of ethical values, an example of moral virtue, and the threat of an evil that lies within the human heart. Surely he adumbrated these very issues in *East of Eden*, but there they are carried by character and plot, not by the sole means of a narrative voice. *America and Americans* turned out to be far more tricky and challenging than anyone would have dreamed when Guinzburg first approached Steinbeck with the project.

In early 1965 Steinbeck pressed hard to finish the essays for *America*. A desire to return to his work on Arthur virtually palpitated in him. With that incentive, he finished the draft in late April. In "Patterns of Reality and Barrels of Worms," Louis Owens argued that Steinbeck's world narrowed and darkened from the time of the Western Flyer to that of Rocinante. If so, he adds, America is a testament to weariness: "*America and Americans* borrows heavily from Steinbeck's previous works and, in spite of Steinbeck's attempts at occasional optimism, documents didactically a darkly patterned reality" (181).[6] If, as Owens asserts, the essays are darkly patterned, then to a large degree the elements that we have considered account for it.

Charley is an account of an author going into the land for rebirth; *America* is more a prolonged question of where is this nation going. John Ditsky strikes the right note, I believe, when he points out that *Charley* is non-teleological, while *America* pursues "a teleology of nationhood" (150). In its philosophical sense, teleology is the study of purposeful development toward an end. The ambiguity of *America* arises from the very indeterminacy of what that end, that *telos*, actually is.

Taking Elaine Steinbeck's comments at the Nantucket conference as her imprimatur, Mimi Gladstein observes that "as the last published work in the man's lifetime, it stands as a capstone and culmination of his career" (228). The claim, however, needs qualification. First, because it is a last work means neither that it is a capstone nor a culmination. In fact, in many respects, *America* is a flawed work that sets it several degrees below his best. Important perhaps; culmination no. Second, in spite of Elaine Steinbeck's and Mimi Gladstein's protestations otherwise, *America* was essentially a work for hire and subject to the narrative limitations discussed earlier in this study. Third, while *America* was the last work published in Steinbeck's lifetime, clearly he did not perceive it to be his last. He was already writing to Elizabeth Otis about publishing the journal he kept while writing *East of Eden*.[7] Furthermore, he looked forward to his work on *Morte D' Arthur*, which clearly he perceived as his culminating work.[8] Nevertheless, *America* is a culmination of sorts—a collection of musings on what the nature, purposes, and ends of this nation are. And this nature, purpose, and end are shaped everywhere by the context of *Morte D' Arthur*.

Not infrequently, Steinbeck pointed out parallels between his own twentieth century and Malory's fifteenth. For example, to Joseph Bryan in 1959, Steinbeck observed that his subject

> has to do with morals. Arthur must awaken not by any means only to repel the enemy from without, but particularly the enemy inside. Immorality is what is destroying us, public immorality. The failure of man toward men, the selfishness that puts making a buck more important than the common weal.

Now, next to our own time the 15th century was the most immoral time we know. Authority was gone. The church split, the monarchy without authority and manorial order disappearing. (Steinbeck and Wallsten 649)

And to Adlai Stevenson in 1959, Steinbeck wrote that he was

back from Camelot, and, reading the papers not at all sure it was wise. Two first impressions. First a creeping, all-pervading, nerve-gas of immorality which starts in the nursery and does not stop before it reaches the highest offices, both corporate and governmental. Two, a nervous restlessness, a hunger, a thirst, a yearning for something unknown—perhaps morality. Then there's the violence, cruelty and hypocrisy symptomatic of a people which has too much, and last the surly, ill-temper which only shows up in humans when they are frightened. (Steinbeck and Wallsten 651–52)

The letter to Stevenson registers as particularly important since, as the letter continues, identical observations appear in *America*.

America, then, examines the shadow of something deeply wrong hovering across the nation. The hortatory tone appears already in the second chapter where Steinbeck berates Americans as a "restless, a dissatisfied, a searching people." One might note the irony of his own compulsion to set out with Charley as born of "the virus of restlessness." But in *America*, Steinbeck quickly qualifies this state as leading to dissatisfaction with the way things are and a relentless struggle to further the self at the expense of others. This indeed leads to a premise held throughout the book. Such dissatisfaction begets injustice, thus revisiting also a central theme of *The Grapes of Wrath*. Surely, many sections of *America* provide clear and penetrating insights that merit re-reading and reflection. The essay on politics and the presidency arises directly from his close relationships with John and Jacqueline Kennedy, Adlai Stevenson, and Lyndon Baines Johnson.

Others stem from prior experience. His essay on African-American equality still feels the sting of the Cheerleaders depicted in *Charley*. The essay on The Corporation Man reads as a gloss on *Winter of Our Discontent*. Discourse begins to slip into diatribe, however, with the essay on how moderns view their children. By the time Steinbeck approaches the topic of Americans and the land, it seems that he is laboring to keep his prose, and emotions, restrained. Nonetheless, the land itself, this beautiful creative mother, wins out in Steinbeck's estimation.

Steinbeck's most baleful analysis arrives when he considers the future. Obsessed with the accumulation of things, he reasons, we have lost the very rules—"ethics, morals, codes of conduct"—that we need to survive. The nation has lapsed into a "bored and slothful cynicism" in which only self-interest serves the individual. We cannot, as a people, reincarnate Camelot, the unity provided by a principled order.

The question of Camelot, never far from Steinbeck's mind in those years, is an intriguing one, for even with the years of study, researching, and translating *Morte*, Steinbeck seems misguided by its central thematic and historical issues. What he did perceive is clear: an heroic but failed effort to stave off the tidal wave of disorder, an inherent nobility that enables a person to rise above dangerous adversaries, and a deeply compelling adventure story. In his February 25, 1964, letter to Jacqueline Kennedy, Steinbeck wrote that

> the 15th century and our own have so much in common—loss of authority, loss of gods, loss of heroes, and loss of lovely pride. When such a hopeless muddled need occurs, it does seem to me that the hungry hearts of men distill their best and truest essence, and that essence becomes a man, and that man a hero so that all men can be reassured that such things are possible. The fact that all of these words—hero, myth, pride, even victory, have been muddied and sicklied by the confusion and pessimism of the times only describes the times. (Steinbeck and Wallsten 793)

A few days later he added, "I do believe that strength and purity tie almost exclusively in the struggle—the becoming (795). Several elements there strike one as contradictory. If strength and purity lie in the struggle, we simple have a Sisyphean cycle with no *telos*. If we have a loss of authority, then what exactly is the authority we have lost? Loss of gods—but exactly what myths does he reference? And what constitutes heroism, or in what may we take pride, for that matter? Steinbeck has eschewed reason for slogans. All of these ideals, as he observed to Mrs. Kennedy, "have been muddied and sicklied by the confusion and pessimism of the times."

In spite of his immersion in Malory, and surely such Arthurian predecessors as Bede, William of Malmesbury, Geoffrey of Monmouth, Wace, and Layamon,[9] Steinbeck misses or disregards several of the essential thematic and ethical issues of these works. Why was this? Three factors emerge. First, while the Arthurian legend in all of its manifestations, at least up through Tennyson's *Idylls*, was perceived as a deeply religious work, Steinbeck perceived it primarily as political. Order for him was not something derived from or imposed by any supreme authority, but something emanating from orderly interaction of humans themselves. Second, while Christological evidence is primary in the legends, and accepted as a de facto reality, Steinbeck perceived the story of Christ on a par with any myth.[10] Finally, Malory's principal concern, largely working as he was from the French *Queste* and the *Alliterative Morte Arthure*, was to understand the massively complicated figure of Lancelot and the conundrum of love, chivalry, and betrayal. This pattern of the Romance, perhaps, formed the primary appeal to Steinbeck's moralistic sensibilities. To set these distinctions concretely, it is helpful to view the moral, social, and political disintegration that Steinbeck asserts in *America* against the very different perceptions of Malory.

In *America and Americans*, Steinbeck concludes in broad strokes that our moral decay originates in our obsession for things, our failure to conserve natural resources, the dominance of the Corporate Man, and our failures in child-rearing, among others. These failures are all self-inflicted and self-perpetuating. Therefore, the corrective arises from a reversal of the primary conditions of our moral collapse by an assertion of human will. Perhaps his own best summary of the ethic appears in Steinbeck's February 28, 1964, letter to Jacqueline Kennedy: "Probably the greatness of our country resides in the fact that we have not made it and are still trying. No—I do believe that strength and purity lie almost exclusively in the struggle—the becoming" (Steinbeck and Wallsten 795).

Malory's vision differs, and is certainly less existential. From its origins, and retained by Malory, the Arthurian legend finds its basis in the concept of Logres. Camelot institutes the city of God and has divine sanction. Chapters 5 to 8 of *Morte* detail the Archbishop of Canterbury's overseeing of Arthur's withdrawal of the sword and his coronation at the Feast of Pentecost. No political figure bestows the honor, but a religious one. The action occurs over the course of the High Holy Days. The sword is withdrawn at Christmas, signifying a divine incarnation in human form. In this case it is Arthur, and the sword is his symbol to order the Round Table, the efficacious agent of his will. Obviously the twelve knights resemble the twelve disciples. At New Year's Day the jousts are celebrated, and from these the first Arthurian knights are selected. At Candlemas (a February 2 feast for the Virgin Mary) Arthur removes the sword yet again before the high lords of Britain. They acclaim him king, but the Archbishop delays until Pentecost, the day of empowerment by the Holy Spirit.[11]

Here, as in earlier versions, the coronation is depicted as a powerfully religious service. The alliterative *Morte Arthure* (c. 1360), with which both Malory and Steinbeck were familiar, describes Arthur thus:

> Than knelis the crownede kynge and kryes levede: "I thanke thee, Gode, of thy grace, with a gud wylle, That gafe us vertue and witt to vencows this beryns And us has grauntede the gree of theis gret lords." (268)

The Logres incarnates the word of God in the political order of the human kingdom. Both the internal and external evidence of Malory's *Morte* provide the sense that Camelot is a spiritual entity, ordered to enact God's will and justice on earth.[12]

Yet that order is violently disrupted, and it is done so through violation of the knightly code of chivalry. In Malory's view, knighthood itself was the worthy and honorable calling of an excellent man. As such, chivalry was the code of deeds for these knights, primarily to enact justice and defend the unprotected. Such accorded perfectly with Steinbeck's view of political order in America. This was the ideal.

Chivalry was at once a moral code and a civil code. Any student of Middle English will recall Chaucer's Knight as the nonpareil of his profession:

> A KNYGHT there was, and that a worthy man, That fro the tyme that he first bigan To riden out, he loved chivalrie, Trouthe and honour, fredom and curteisie. (43–46)

In contemporary language, we may translate those qualities of the Code of Chivalry as follows: Pledging fidelity (troth), acting honorably, valuing freedom of others, and following the social order of courtesy. Chivalry is thereby a civil and spiritual code manifested in the behavior of the knight in Logres. Furthermore, herein lies the ethical framework of the Arthurian legends—predicated communal beliefs effect committed individual actions.

Precisely here Malory ran into difficulty, and this is the essential issue that I believe either escaped Steinbeck or that he simply ignored. Moreover, this ethics of communal belief and committed action is absolutely essential to the whole legendary material with which Steinbeck worked in his translation. For Malory, the supreme paradox was this: how could Lancelot, most gallant of the knights, pervert his gallantry in his sin with Guinevere? While the French *Queste* condemns the sin and requires penance of Lancelot, Malory persists in describing Lancelot's intentional virtue. To the end, Malory insists that Lancelot was "the best of any synfull man of the worlde" (863). Malory thereby relativizes both the sin of Lancelot and the ethics of chivalry to something like "doing the best you can." Indeed, Lancelot supplants any spiritual goal with this one earthly and relative goal:

> And all my grete dedis of armys that I have done for the moste party was all for the quenys sake, and for hir sake wolde I do batayle were hit ryght other wronge. *And never dud I batayle all only for Goddis sake, but for to wynne worship and to cause me the bettir to be beloved, and litill or nought I thanked never God of hit.* [emphasis mine] (897)

What Malory attempts to forge is a bifurcated ethic. When done in the name of Camelot, Lancelot's mighty deeds are blameless. When done self-interestedly, they are blameworthy. But neither Lancelot nor Malory can have it so. The affair with Guinevere is simply wrong, and, as Lancelot confesses, it occurred because he transferred loyalty from God to the Queen. Consequently, Logres shatters. Humanity now lies, as Steinbeck recognized, East of Eden.

There are no roadmaps back. In spite of Lancelot's valiant but self-maddening redemptive effort to find the Grail, he is not permitted. Nor can he accept that he cannot. The crack in Camelot widens and neither Lancelot nor all the king's men can ever put Camelot together again.

In the ever-depressing and devolving litany of failure articulated in *America and Americans*, Steinbeck oddly places his optimism in humanity. One finds a sense of Hegelian progress—out of dialectic we can't go back and we do stumble, sometimes unwittingly, along a road called the future. Essentially, Steinbeck's ethics in *America* is thoroughly postmodern and relativist. Our strength and salvation arises from within ourselves. It had better, or we are doomed. The ethical problem should be readily apparent. Who is to say whose strength is right or wrong? Steinbeck laments the passing of the old virtues and codes of conduct, but says little about how to establish new ones. Against the waning of Camelot into the glooming dark, Steinbeck finds few bulwarks except an optimistic faith in humanity itself.

Elaine Steinbeck made a telling remark to conclude her April 1993 interview with Donald and Mary Jeanne Coers at her Manhattan apartment. Don Coers had just remarked on Steinbeck's "fundamental faith in democracy and human decency." To which Elaine responded:

"You see, John believed in man. That's what his Nobel Prize speech says. He said, 'You believe in the perfectibility of man. Man will never be perfect, but he has to strive for it.' That's the whole point. That was his whole point about life" (271). In a sense, Steinbeck stands ethically side by side with Lancelot in the ruins of Camelot. One battles on, doing the best one can, before the darkness falls.

NOTES

1. See Stephen George, ed. *The Moral Philosophy of John Steinbeck*. Lanham, Maryland: Scarecrow, 2005, 228.

2. Elaine's comment also surfaced publicly during the next day of meetings. Mimi Reisel Gladstein recalls the event: "After hearing one speaker too many refer to *America and Americans* as a cocktail table book, she got up to voice her displeasure. That was not, she assured us, how John viewed the book. It was, she explained, an important undertaking for him and he had put much work and thought into the project" (228).

3. First published together as a pamphlet, *Their Blood is Strong* in 1938, and then again in 1988 under the original title *The Harvest Gypsies* by Heyday Books.

4. In "Patterns of Reality and Barrels of Worms," Louis Owens makes keen distinctions between *Sea of Cortez* and *Charley*. To the point here, Owens writes, "The patterned reality of the *Log* cannot merely give Steinbeck his own reflection as will be the case when, in *Travels with Charley*, the shaping consciousness will be Steinbeck's alone" (174).

5. Mixed into this was Steinbeck's invitation to draft the 1964 inauguration speech for Lyndon Baines Johnson. He halted writing on *America* to undertake the work, only to discover later that nearly all his work wound up on "the room floor." See Benson, *John Steinbeck, Writer*, pp. 961–62.

6. In her essay "Reading Steinbeck (Re)-Reading America," Geralyn Strecker lays side by side parallel passages first appearing in *Charley* and then in *America*.

7. *Journal of a Novel* was published posthumously in 1969.

8. In the same essay, Gladstein very tellingly ties together the work on *Morte* and the contextual tenor of *America*, the subject of my further discussion.

9. The list also includes T. R. White's *Once and Future King*, which Steinbeck called "a marvelously wrought work" (Steinbeck and Wallsten 633).

10. Regarding the nature of Christ, sometimes Steinbeck grudgingly admits his historicity, but in his later years settled into the belief that he is simply a mythic icon:

> Where does the myth—the legend—start? Back of the Celtic version it stretches back to India and probably before. The people of legend are not people as we know them. They are figures. Christ is not a person, he is a figure. Buddha is a

squatting symbol. As a person Malory's Arthur is a fool. As a legend he is time-less. You can't explain him in human terms any more than you can explain Jesus. (Steinbeck and Wallsten 633)

11. One of Steinbeck's most direct testaments of rejection of religion oc-curs in a March 30, 1959, letter to Elizabeth Otis:

Yesterday, Easter, we went to services in the Bruton church. I found it nostalgically moving because I knew it all from my childhood, but also I found again that there is nothing in it that I need or want. Elaine both needs and wants it and so she may have it. But I'll take my birds any day and the processional of the sun. (Steinbeck and Wallsten 623)

12. In a neatly inverse pattern in *The Winter of Our Discontent*, Ethan Hawley's moral descent occurs over passion week. Hawley's descent into hell during the spiritual center of Easter weekend should make a strong ethical statement. But Hawley is hardly the one to do it. Unlike Arthur or Lancelot, Hawley shows from the start little intrinsic nobility. He evidences no point of moral authority from which to fall. He is essentially insipid, save for the fact that he is infected by a virus of amorality. He does not so much fall as simply topple over.

WORKS CITED

(Anon.) *Alliterative Morte Arthure* (c. 1360). *Middle English Literature*. Ed. Charles W. Dunn and Edward T. Byrnes. New York: Harcourt Brace Jova-novich, 1973.

Benson, Jackson J. *John Steinbeck, Writer*. New York: Viking, 1984.

Chaucer, Geoffrey. *The Works of Geoffrey Chaucer*. Ed. F.N. Robinson. Boston: Houghton Mifflin, 1961.

Ditsky, John. "Steinbeck's *Travels with Charley*: The Quest that Failed." *Stein-beck's Travel Literature: Essays in Criticism*. Ed. Tetsumaro Hayashi. Steinbeck Monograph Series, No. 10. Muncie: Steinbeck Society, 1980: 55–61.

George, Stephen, Ed. *The Moral Philosophy of John Steinbeck*. Lanham, MD: Scarecrow Press, 2005.

Gladstein, Mimi Reisel. "*America and Americans*: The Arthurian Consumma-tion." *After* The Grapes of Wrath: *Essays on John Steinbeck in Honor of Tet-sumaro Hayashi*. Ed. Donald V. Coers, et al. Athens: Ohio University Press, 1995: 228–37.

Malory, Sir Thomas. *Le Morte D' Arthur*. In *The Works of Thomas Malory*. Ed. Eugene Vinaver. Oxford: Oxford University Press, 1929, 1959.

Owens, Louis. "Patterns of Reality and Barrels of Worms: From Western Flyer to Rocinante in Steinbeck's Fiction." *The Steinbeck Question: New Essays in*

Criticism. Ed. Donald R. Noble. Troy, New York: The Whitston Publishing Co., 1993, 171–82.

Steinbeck, Elaine. "John Believed in Man: An Interview with Mrs. John Steinbeck." In *After* The Grapes of Wrath, 241–271.

Steinbeck, Elaine and Robert Wallsten. Ed. *Steinbeck: A Life in Letters.* New York: Viking, 1975.

Steinbeck, John. *America and Americans.* New York: Viking Press, 1966.

———. *The Harvest Gypsies: On the Road to* The Grapes of Wrath. Berkeley, CA: Heyday Books, 1988.

———. *Sea of Cortez.* New York: Viking, 1941.

———. *Travels with Charley: In Search of America.* New York: Viking, 1962.

———. *The Winter of Our Discontent.* New York: Viking, 1961.

Strecker, Geralyn. "Reading Steinbeck (Re)-Reading America: *Travels with Charley* and *America and Americans.*" In *After* The Grapes of Wrath, 214–227.

Part 3

STEINBECK, THE EYES OF A CHILD, AND LONELY LADIES

Few authors are adept at creating children as full characters. Usually, they either write children's books, or keep child characters on the periphery of their stories. Steinbeck is a notable exception, who was able to invoke a sense of his boyhood, delve into his immature memory banks, and create children who ring true.

—Mimi Gladstein

Though neither author delivers conclusive conflict resolutions, Steinbeck more clearly than Welty blames the male's obsession with female purity for the loneliness and neurosis of humankind.

—Charlotte Hadella

6

Through the Eyes of a Child

A Steinbeck Forte

Mimi Reisel Gladstein
The University of Texas at El Paso

> The child is father of the man.
>
> —William Wordsworth

Wordsworth's poetic observation is an apt introduction to an exploration of the source for one of John Steinbeck's most intriguing writing fortes, his ability to create convincing and charming child characters. Certainly, one needs to look only cursorily into Steinbeck's childhood to find the parent of that particular creative ability. His early fascination with the Arthurian myth, inspired by the gift of *Morte d'Arthur*, is what he credits with opening for him a "magic" world and inspiring a "passionate love of the English language" (Benson 21). It also sparked an imaginative ardor that carried through his entire creative life; he was working on a contemporary language version of Malory's work when he died.[1] John and his sister Mary played Knights and Squires, fancying their pony Jill in the role of a gallant steed. Steinbeck maintained that imaginative part of himself throughout his life, and one way it manifested itself was in his ability to get into the mindset of his child characters while at the same time maintaining an appropriate authorial distance.

Few authors are adept at creating children as full characters. Usually, they either write children's books, or keep child characters on the periphery of their stories. Steinbeck is a notable exception, who was able to invoke a sense of his boyhood, delve into his immature memory banks, and create children who ring true. Steinbeck's children are sentient creatures who experience and think about the world as children, thus appealing to the child in the reader, while at the same time avoiding the all too convenient trap of falling into the good child/bad child stereotypes. Steinbeck's children are also notable for what they are not: they are neither miniature adults nor literary objects to be manipulated to expose some underlying statement about existence that the author wishes to reveal.[2]

Jody Tiflin of *The Red Pony* stories may be among the best-drawn children in American literature. And, in keeping with that special quality of Steinbeck's creation of child characters, the novel is at once a book for children and a book for adults. An analysis of Steinbeck's techniques in creating Jody can serve as entry to a study of some of the other examples of this skill. One of the most charmingly evocative scenes depicting a child's magical world of the imagination comes early in "The Promise," third of the four stories that form *The Red Pony.* The skill that Steinbeck handles so masterfully is maintaining in the reader the sense that one is in Jody's mind, although it is not a first person narrative. The scene is set as Jody is coming home from school, creating in his mind's eye a panorama of martial splendor. Steinbeck humorously tells the reader that Jody "marched seemingly alone," but that "behind him there was a phantom army with great flags and swords, silent but deadly" (256). The trick here is that the reader is at once objectively surveying a scene of a solitary walk and at the same time invited into Jody's imaginative world. The experience of pretending a bucket or pail is a drum and creating sound effects by fluttering a tongue "sharply against his teeth to fill in snare drums and occasional trumpets" (256) is almost universal. Steinbeck brings all of Nature into this imaginative scene as "animals stopped their feeding and their play" (257) to watch Jody's phantom gray and silent army march by. Steinbeck maintains the fantasy particularly artfully in this scene even after Jody's attention is diverted to a horny toad. He amuses the reader by maintaining the army illusion, so that when Jody loses interest, we are tickled to read that the army "halted, bewildered and nervous." As Jody becomes intrepid hunter rather than army drum major, the army stands in "long uneasy ranks for a moment and then, with a soft sigh of sorrow, rose up in a faint gray mist and disappeared" (257). Quickly, we are moved to the next flight of Jody's fancy as a "long gray rifle" appears in his right hand and a "new and unexpected population of gray tigers and grey bears" roam the brush along the road (257). By the time Jody reaches home he had "captured two more horny-toads, four little grass lizards, a blue snake, sixteen yellow-winged grasshoppers and a brown damp newt." While many female readers may not associate with this experience, the males in Steinbeck's readership will probably be provoked to happy memories of their own days as scourges upon the insect and small creature population. This section of the story is handled for nostalgic and comic effect, but those are not the only tones in Steinbeck's multi-hued pallet of child characterization.

Steinbeck is also particularly good at conveying the nuances of the parent/child relationship from the perspective of both parties. Anyone who has had strict parents can associate the sense of subconscious guilt Jody displays when his mother tells him his father wants to talk to him. "Do you—is it something I did" (259)? Of course, the perpetually guilty conscience is well earned, as the narrator humorously reminds the reader. Jody has left all the creepy, crawly things he collected in his role as the big game hunter in his lunchbox and "conscientiously" hurries to the barn to see his father, ignoring his mother's gasp of rage when she opens it. Steinbeck also shows Jody's sensitivity to his father's ire. When Carl Tiflin is cruel to Grandfather, Jody empathizes: "Jody knew how he felt, how his insides were collapsed and empty" (296).

Steinbeck develops Jody in full humanity, never allowing him to become a cliché or stock character. Jody is fleshed out as a totally rounded character, by turns thoughtful, but still full of childlike carelessness. Steinbeck is particularly effective with creating those little touches of paradoxical realness as the boy does things that boys often do, but shouldn't. Walking through the vegetable garden in "The Gift," Jody can't resist the urge to "smash a green muskmelon with his heel." At the same time, the thoughtful part of him knows that "it was a bad thing to do," and so he "kicked dirt over the ruined melon to conceal it" (205). Steinbeck sprinkles the text with other such instances of that ornery or mischievous quality in children that leads them to tromp in new shoes through every mud puddle on a road when there is plenty of space to walk around them.

Jody's characterization is broad and detailed, and as a fully developed male child, he is not spared his share of that thoughtless and insensate cruelty that little boys often exhibit. Doubletree Mutt is

often his victim. In "The Gift" Steinbeck captures Jody's appropria-
tion of the dog as a scapegoat for his pain and frustration at not being
able to cure the pony's illness. When the dog comes into the barn,
wagging his tail, "incensed at his health" Jody throws a hard black
clod at him (231), later feeling guilty about his cruel act. On other
occasions, the narrator notes that more often than not, it is not cruelty that motivates the boy's sadistic behavior, but boredom (238).
"The Great Mountains" begins on a warm summer day when there is
nothing going on and Jody has nothing to do. So, first he kills time by
destroying swallows' nests and then baiting a mousetrap with cheese
so that Doubletree Mutt would get his nose snapped in it. Jody then
gets a slingshot and kills a little thrush, which he then disembowels
and cuts up, disposing of the parts, not because he cares about the life
of the bird, but because he knows the killing of the bird would reflect
negatively on him with older people and therefore "he was ashamed
because of their potential opinion" (240).

In "The Great Mountains" the child Jody is privileged as none of the
adults, even Billy Buck who is sensitive to Gitano's dignity, in that he
has more information than they have. Whereas the adults in the Tiflin
family are not particularly pleased at the arrival of Gitano, the old
paisano, the narrator describes Jody's reaction to the man's statement
that he has returned to the ranch with subtle humor. "Jody could not
take all this responsibility" (244) and he runs for help. He reports the
fact to his mother "excitedly." Later, Jody's sense of the romance of the
stranger is rewarded when Gitano shows him the "lean and lovely rapier with a golden basket hilt" (253). Jody is the only one who knows
of the rapier, a symbol of Gitano's noble past, and though he does
not understand his reactions, has pieces of the puzzle and mystery of
Old Gitano that he does not share with the adults. Mr. Tiflin knows
only that Gitano has taken Old Easter and is pleased that it will "save
me burying that horse" (255). Both Mr. Tiflin and Jess Taylor mistake
the glint of the rapier's steel, as seen from afar, for a gun. It is through
Jody's perception that the reader is able to piece together the sweep
of generational drama that harks back to forgotten noble and landed
ancestors and forward to a boy feeling "a longing" and a "nameless
sorrow," but not understanding what he has experienced.

"A Leader of the People," originally the title of a separate short story
in the *Long Valley* collection, was subsequently published as the last
of the four sections of the book *The Red Pony*. Steinbeck's mastery in
the creation of child characters is never more tellingly demonstrated.

This may be because, for this story, Steinbeck presents Jody in a transitional state, a state where he learns compassion and caring behavior.³ Steinbeck opens with a description of one of those archetypal boy-like behaviors, "Jody tramped down scuffing his shoes in a way he had been told was destructive to good shoe-leather" (283). Every parent will recognize the phenomenon. Watching Billy Buck work with the haystack, Jody is anxious to begin a mouse hunt. In his imagination the mice are "plump, sleek, arrogant" and "smug"(294). Doom awaits them.⁴ Subtle detail characterizes Steinbeck's development of Jody's character. Expressing his hope that it will not rain till after the mouse hunt, Jody references the little creatures as "those damn mice," checking to see the effect of his "mature profanity" (285). Again, Steinbeck taps an archetypal experience of childhood, the first conscious use of profanity around an adult. The arrival of Mrs. Tiflin's father, whose recounting of the pioneer days of California history enchants Jody but bores the grown-ups, is played with quintessential Steinbeck perceptiveness. Here Jody, whose insensitivities have been displayed earlier in the narrative, anticipates his grandfather's feelings and, notwithstanding his father's annoyance at the coming visit, suggests that he go up the road to meet his grandfather. His mother expresses her approval, "That would be nice. . . . He'd probably like to be met" (289). With his characteristic psychological insight into the paradoxical nature of this period in a boy's life, Steinbeck includes details that illustrate growing adult compassion mixed with holdovers from the little boy behaviors. When he first sights his grandfather, Jody races down the road to meet him, trying "to leap into the middle of his shadow at every step" (290), but, once in sight of his grandfather he changes from his "unseemly running" and approaches "at a dignified walk" (290). When Jody goes to bed, after the evening meal and Grandfather's retelling of his adventures, before he falls asleep, he fantasizes about living in those heroic times.

The next morning, however, Steinbeck foreshadows Jody's gradual maturation by his reaction to a philosophical comment by Billy Buck. Jody is "staggered" (299) by Billy's response to his observation that the intended victims of his mouse hunt, "don't know what's going to happen to them today." Billy Buck observes that neither he nor Jody do either, "nor anyone" (299). Pondering the profundity of this thought is one of the stepping-stones Steinbeck provides to anticipate Jody's later development in the story. His ability to think outside himself prefigures his slow maturation. Steinbeck develops in Jody an ability to empathize, a telling bridge to a more adult human being. In this part of the narrative, Steinbeck is most masterful. Jody's empathy is developing, but he has only his childlike tools with which to express it, making him all the more endearing as a character. Grandfather, whose feelings have been hurt by Carl Tiflin, cannot summon the effort to participate in Jody's mouse hunt. Jody sees him sitting on the porch "looking small and thin and black" (302) and quickly loses his own enthusiasm. As his grandfather speaks of the loss of the Westering spirit in people, Jody's only ameliorating tool is to offer a glass of lemonade. Acknowledgment of Jody's maturing empathy expressed with this little boy tool is emphasized by his mother, who at first mistakes his desire to make lemonade for his grandfather as a childish manipulation to get one for himself, but whose dawning realization of the situation causes her to conclude the story with the soft, "Here, I'll reach the squeezer down to you" (304).

Though Jody is the only named child character in the stories that comprise *The Red Pony*, Steinbeck does not limit himself to this single depiction of the workings of a child's mind. One particularly effective passage occurs in "The Gift," where the narrator explains the result of Jody's acquisition of a horse. Steinbeck does not settle for a surface explication of one child's jealousy of another child's having something he or she covets. Instead the narrator explains the special nature of Jody's gift, the psychological and archetypal layers beneath the attitude of the other children toward Jody, their new respect: "Out of the thousand centuries they drew the ancient admiration of the footman for the horseman" (211). The narration explains that Jody's possession of a horse has lifted him both literally and figuratively above them. Steinbeck's creation of the scene in which the boys all jockey for a position that will allow them to eventually ride the pony is a gem of its kind, concluding as "each boy, in his mind, searched among his possessions for a bribe worthy of offering in return for a ride on the red pony when the time should come" (212).

Jody is the most fully and expertly drawn of Steinbeck's child characters, but there are notable others. Though a World War and two marriages intervene between the creation of Jody and the boys, Aron and Cal, in *East of Eden*, Steinbeck is able to maintain his keen insight into the minds of children. Steinbeck's personal family inspiration for these characters is well documented.[5] Cal is the focus of most of Steinbeck's narrative attention, and his function in the generational plot line cannot be more important. He is the key to the future. It is through him that Steinbeck is attempting to send a message not only to his sons, but also to his readers.[6] As he set about his task, Steinbeck was not unmindful of his particular talents in the area of child characterization. In *Journal of a Novel*, he writes, quoting his character Lee, "I think adults forget about children. They just literally do not remember how it was. *I think I do remember* and I am going to try very hard to remember more" (198). Later in the journal he returns to the subject, noting, "Most of what I read about children is crap. Grown people forget. . . . And so I will set it down and I think it will be an unique record of the thinking of children" (200). Furthermore, Steinbeck was sensitive to the trap of creating cliché child characters. He observes that "children are no more alike than are adults" (200). Aron, Cal, and Abra are individuated and carefully developed.

Returning to the Wordsworthian concept of the child as father to the man, it can be stated that it was not until *East of Eden* that Steinbeck set himself the task of developing a character all the way from birth to adulthood. It is part and parcel of his "timshel" theme that although the child brings to adulthood much of its genetic background as well as the nurturing or lack of nurturing it receives, in the end, each human can make a choice—*timshel*, thou mayest.

The twins, Aron and Cal, are not introduced to the reader as sentient beings until the novel is a little more than half over. They are eleven years old and in their first scene, Steinbeck immediately establishes the individuality of these two boys, characterizing Cal as aggressive and manipulative. Cal not only tries to pick a fight with his brother, but he also seeks to disillusion him about their absent mother—Aron wants to believe that she is dead, whereas Cal has overheard some men saying she ran away (388). Steinbeck is neither romantic nor sentimental in his portrayal of the boy Cal. He is a round character, with both his negative and positive qualities displayed. The narrator lets us know that Cal, seeing Aron's strong reaction to the idea that the romanticized stories about their mother may not be true, realizes that he has a new tool against his brother and that "he could bring it out anytime and he knew it was the sharpest weapon he had found" (389). Painting Cal as Machiavellian one minute and all boy the next, Steinbeck's keen portrayal ends the scene with Cal and Aron running and laughing in a sudden rainstorm, as they throw the rabbit they have killed back and forth.

When Abra is introduced into the equation, Steinbeck invests the scene with his characteristic humorous tone as the boys vie for her attentions and cope with the arrival of a female presence into their hitherto masculine sphere. Cal suddenly offers her the rabbit he and/or Aron had killed. Of course, Steinbeck well remembers that what is treasure to a male child may be trash to the female, and Abra responds, "What would I want with a dirty old rabbit all covered with blood?" Aron propitiates this new deity by offering to put the rabbit in a box and suggesting a funeral for it. With the psychological aptitude that most children display, Abra senses that she is in charge and she inspects "her conquests" (398). When her inquiries reveal that they are motherless, the narrator tells us that Abra "drew on her fairy tales" and immediately jumps to a variety of conclusions. She asks if their father beats them, if they sit in ashes and fetch water and faggots. Steinbeck draws on the humor of her use of fairy tale vocabulary, a language unknown to the boys and Aron asks, "What's faggots?" (399). As he had for Jody in *The Red Pony*, Steinbeck humorously creates for the reader the child's imaginative world. In Abra's mind she had, considering the boys' raggedy clothes and disheveled looks, cast them in a sort of male Cinderella story with her as their fairy godmother, but when she uncovers no wicked stepmother, as the narrator tells us, her fantasy is not permanently destroyed, and she quickly adopts another in which she wears "a big hat with an ostrich plume and she carried an enormous basket from which a turkey's feet protruded" (399).

Steinbeck deftly moves from the charm of this scene to an exploration of Cal's personality, in particular the tools he has developed to cope with the fact that people prefer his brother Aron. In response Cal has learned to punish those who prefer Aron, and he brandishes his weapons on Abra. That children can be cruel is common knowledge, but Steinbeck probes into the subconscious reasons for that cruelty and peals away the layers of both cause and effect. As the narrator explains it, "Out of revenge Cal extracted a fluid of power, and out of power, joy" (401). As Aron is the root cause for Cal's "feelings of triumph," Cal loves Aron, not remembering "if he had ever known" that the reason for his sadistic acts is that he wants to be loved as Aron is (401). The scene ends with Aron's feeling sadly crushed by what he perceives as Abra's rejection, a perception cunningly contrived by Cal. What Steinbeck does so skillfully with the character of Cal is to make him at once repulsive and attractive. As the Cain figure, the one whose gifts are rejected by the deity, he is at once an individual and a representative for Everyone since we are all the descendants of Cain. In the

Bible and in the novel, Abel dies without issue. It is interesting that Steinbeck chooses a Cain figure for his final protagonist in this novel. Conventional symbolism casts Cain as a villain, a fratricide, and an outcast. Over a century earlier, Lord Byron had made a similar choice, making Cain the protagonist for a play of the same name. Like Byron, Steinbeck provides the rationales for Cain's destructive actions.

An attribute of children that Steinbeck captures effectively in a number of his characterizations is their excitement at anything out of the ordinary, anything that is a disruption of routine. My favorite in this area is his description in *The Grapes of Wrath* of Ruthie and Winfield at the prospect of killing the pigs in preparation for the trip to California. With a minimum of verbiage, he communicates the children's reaction. He describes their "hopping excitedly . . . like crazy things" (133). Maintaining the metaphor of their out-of-proportion reaction, the narrator describes Winfield as "reduced to madness" (133). He must act out the hideous prospect of killing the pig, miming cutting his throat, making a horrible face, and sinking to the ground in the death throes.

In his characterization of these children, particularly Winfield, Steinbeck reminds us that what to adults may be tragic or disgusting, is often a source of great excitement to the children. When, on their trek to California. the group makes a rest stop, Ruthie and Winfield go exploring. Ruthie finds gray snake eggs, which she is at first excited about; but when she realizes that the adults do not find her prize significant, she throws them away. In the meantime, she and Winfield spot a dead dog on the side of the road. Winfield is immediately animated by the gore, first exclaiming excitedly, "His guts was just strowed all over—all over . . . strowed—all—over" (168). Then the reality of the scene hits him and he vomits down the side of the truck.

Ruthie and Winfield perform an important function in the theme of *The Grapes of Wrath*. As the youngest members of the Joad clan, they represent the future. But, in terms of plot, their role is small for much of the novel, although Ruthie serves to initiate the climactic separation of Tom from the family. Again Steinbeck's acute understanding of a child's psychology makes the scene ring true. After Ruthie and Winfield have been given the unusual treat of a cracker-jack box each, Ruthie, who, child-like is trying to make her box last as long as possible by cutting the popcorn morsels in half, is accosted by some children. After some fighting, Ruthie reacts with a time-tested childish taunt that her brother would kill the brother of the big girl who beat her.[7] Then she brags that her brother "already kil't two fellas." The girl responds that Ruthie is a liar, and Ruthie tells about Tom's hiding from the law. The scene captures the child's lack of comprehension of the full impact of her actions. Of course, Winfield plays the typical younger sibling, anxious to tell on her and hopeful that she will be punished, asking, "Gonna whup her, Ma?" (529). While the reader's reaction may be somewhat like Pa's who exclaims, "Why, the little bitch" when he learns that she told, Ma reminds the reader that Ruthie's behavior is typical for a child, that she did not realize what she had done. Of course, Winfield is anxious to communicate to Ruthie the enormity of her sin, and once again tries to encourage Ma to "whup her." Tom, when Ma tells him, empathizes and recalls his childish behavior, "With me I was always gonna get Uncle John after 'em . . . . That's jus' kid talk" (534).

Steinbeck does not succumb to the temptation to make Ruthie's transgression a learning experience for her. Rather, he maintains his authorial objectivity and continues to portray her realistically. At the end of the novel, with disaster after disaster befalling the family, she is still child enough to whine and complain when the continual rain keeps them cooped up in the boxcar. Unmindful of the flood dangers and solipsistic as ever, Ruthie and Winfield continue their bickering until almost the last page of the novel.

The relish with which Steinbeck recreates days of innocence and lack of responsibility is not surprising. A recurring theme in many of his major works is nostalgia for a pre-lapsarian Edenic world, a world of boyish men, men without the civilizing or disturbing effect of women. *Cannery Row* is the quintessential example. Given the homeless, jobless, and generally devil-may-care state of most of the characters in this novel, it is not surprising that there are few children portrayed; these are not family men, nor is *Cannery Row* a family-friendly atmosphere. It is testament to Steinbeck's subtlety of characterization that the main child character evokes pathos rather than humor. This is Frankie, the awkward boy who begins hanging out at Western Biological when he is eleven. Steinbeck's works display great sympathy for the outcasts of society, the ones who do not fit, particularly those that are born impaired. Most of these mentally or physically handicapped characters are grown, the most famous being Lennie in *Of Mice and Men*. Frankie, like Tularecito in *The Pastures of Heaven*, is of school age, but there is no place for him in a school system and society that don't know what to do with him. And although some hard-bitten critics have found Steinbeck guilty of sentimentality, his characterization of Frankie is anything but. The reader must read between the lines to assess the wretchedness of the boy's home situation. When Doc asks him why he hangs around the lab, he replies, "You don't hit me or give me a nickel" (35). Doc learns that Frankie is not wanted at school because he "couldn't learn and there was something a little wrong with his coordination" (35). Frankie's father is dead and his mother has probably taken up prostitution. When Doc asks Frankie who hits him or gives him nickels, his answer is "the uncles" who are always around the house. Doc buys Frankie new clothes, feeds him and lets him help around the laboratory. Naturally, all the kindness to an abused and neglected boy earns Frankie's devotion.

But, Steinbeck does not opt for the happy-ever-after solution to Frankie's problems. In both chapters that feature him, there are sad endings. The easy, happy-go-lucky life of the Row does not extend to Frankie. Though the reader is never exactly sure of the diagnosis for Frankie's mental and physical problems, Steinbeck adroitly reconstructs a thinking process for Frankie through which he has accomplished something to help Doc and wants to repeat the act. At a small party, Frankie had taken a drink to one of the women guests, eliciting thanks from her and praise from Doc. Thus, at a larger party, he attempts a whole tray of drinks and unhappily, "the coordination failed, the hands fumbled, the panicked muscles, the nerves, telegraphed to a dead operator, the response did not come back" (37). One of the reason's Steinbeck's portrayal of children is so skillful is that he neither sentimentalizes nor romanticizes his portrayals. One might say he does not opt for fairy tale endings, but maybe, that is exactly what he does. "The Little Match Girl" freezes to death and "The Little Mermaid" lives a life of pain when she gives up her fishtail. Doc finds Frankie whimpering and alone after the drink debacle and realizes that "there wasn't a thing in the world he could do" (37).

A complete analysis of all of the children Steinbeck created in his long and varied career is beyond the scope of this essay, but I would be remiss in this discussion of Steinbeck's gift with creating child characters if I did not include Robbie, the delightful child in the "Junius Maltby" chapter in *Pastures of Heaven*. Ostensibly, the chapter is about Junius, the father, and his attempt to find a haven in the Pastures community. Robbie, however, steals the show. This is not to say that Junius, in his own way, is any less of a child than his son. Like so many of the other exemplars of Steinbeck's disdain for middle-class values—

especially work and responsibility—Junius is happy. "He was content to sit in the sun and to dangle his feet in the stream (89). Thematically, the Maltby story is almost Byronic in its exemplification of the knowledge-is-sorrow thesis. As long as Junius does not know his neighbor's feelings about him, he is content; as long as Robbie does not know he is an object of pity, he is a natural leader among the boys.

Pastures of Heaven is one of Steinbeck's earlier works, but in it, as he was to demonstrate later in *The Red Pony*, he shows his particularly adept hand at portraying the hierarchies among boys. In *The Red Pony* Jody does not attain his status because of anything he has done or his natural leadership; he has it because he has something (the pony) that all the boys covet. In the Junius Maltby story, the narrator does not explain why, but the reader comes to understand that because of Robbie's inherent innocence and natural charisma, all the boys who were predisposed to taunt him or make fun of his clothes, become instead his friends and followers. The fact that the younger boys imitate him, "even tearing holes in the knees of their overalls" is a description that probably had more impact on the reader in those Depression Days when torn clothes were not the fashion statement they are now. The same can be said for Robbie's long and unkempt hair. Robbie enchants his schoolmates in much the same way Scheherazade enthralled her sultan; Robbie captures the attention of his peers with his story telling. He reads them *Treasure Island* while they sit on the sycamore branch and tells them about the Gallic Wars and the Battle of Trafalgar. Robbie becomes "the king of the school yard" (92).

Steinbeck delights readers as he explores the adventures of a boy brought up in the oral world of storytelling having to cope with learning the written word. Of course, Robbie's adult vocabulary, rather than making him an object of scorn, adds to his prestige in the context of setting up the Boys Auxiliary Secret Service For Espionage Against the Japanese. The narrator explains that after Robbie uses such words as "behoofs" and "nefarious," the would-be members of the group "succumbed before this glorious diction" (95).[8]

Much of the story recalls the fun and frolic attendant to childhood adventures, a make-believe world where even Miss Morgan, the teacher, is captured by the fantasy as the boys rescue the President from being burned at the stake by the Indians. Entering into the play, when Junius tells her he is not Mr. Maltby, but three hundred Indians, she moves obediently out of the way so she will not be massacred. Giving in to and participating in the fantasy, she achieves such exalted status that "the boys had ceased to regard her as the teacher" (100). Of course the days of rescuing the President and hanging the culprits give way to school boards and do-gooders. Although Miss Morgan tries to prevent it, the Munroes, in seeking to help, destroy the Edenic world of the Maltbys. When Robbie bolts from the gift of new clothes, Miss Morgan explains that Robbie never knew he was poor until they try to treat him like a charity case. Knowledge brings sorrow as it does for Adam and Eve in Genesis. The story ends with Junius and Robbie, cast out of their garden, going to San Francisco, where Junius will become an accountant and Robbie will probably become like every other boy.

Recalling his father in an interview article for *John Steinbeck: A Centennial Tribute*, Thom Steinbeck remembers him as "so wonderfully boyish" (4). He also tells the story that all the neighborhood children, who adored his father, would "come over and ask Elaine if he could come out and play" (4). Thom opines that one of the reasons was that his father never talked down to them. That quality evidences itself in Steinbeck's development of his child characters. He neither disrespects his child characters by making them less realistic than his adult characters, nor does he talk down to his readers by creating contrived or cliché child characters. Struggling with characterization as he was writing *East of Eden*, Steinbeck writes Pat Covici: "I think I am making people of these children and this I must do. They must be real people" (177). And that, I would argue, is one of the reasons that Steinbeck's children ring true to the reader. He clearly understood that to create a credible child character, he had to tap into the child in himself and remember the thoughts and the feelings of children. He was careful, as he wrote in *Journal of a Novel*, to write children not "as they are conceived by adults but children as they are to and among themselves" (200). This he was able to accomplish admirably, maintaining his insights from the days of his early stories through the decades of success and aging.

NOTES

1. Numerous critics have noted the resonance of Arthurian themes throughout Steinbeck's writing career. See, for example, Kinney, Arthur F. "The Arthurian Cycle in *Tortilla Flat*," *Steinbeck: A Collection of Critical Essays*, ed. Robert Murray Davis, Englewood Cliff: Prentice-Hall, 1972, 36–46; Gladstein, Mimi

R. "*America and Americans*: The Arthurian Consummation," *After 'The Grapes of Wrath': Essays on John Steinbeck in honor of Tetsumaro Hayashi*, Eds. Donald V. Coers, Paul D. Ruffin, Robert J. DeMott. Athens: Ohio University Press, 1995, 228–37. French, Warren. *John Steinbeck*. New Haven: Twayne, 1961, 53–61.

2. Credit is due Juan Sybert-Coronado whose response to an assignment in a Hemingway and Steinbeck graduate seminar was the catalyst for this paper.

3. I have explored this transition in "The Leader of the People: A Boy Becomes a Mench," *Steinbeck's The Red Pony: Essays in Criticism*, ed. Tetsumaro Hayashi and Thomas J. Moore, (Steinbeck Monograph Series), No. 13, 1988, 27–37.

4. The heedless mouse metaphor was evidently in Steinbeck's consciousness at this time. The year before, he had used an allusion to Burns' "To a Mouse" as the title for *Of Mice and Men*. The message of disaster falling regardless of our best laid plans is close to what Jody thinks of for the mice.

5. *Journal of a Novel*, the posthumously published letters to his friend and editor Pascal Covici, details his concerns with his two sons and his original intention to write the book to them.

6. I have argued elsewhere about the mixed nature of that message. After all, he had two sons and in this paradigm, only one survives. See "Friendly Fire: Steinbeck's *East of Eden*," *The Betrayal of Brotherhood in the Work of John Steinbeck*, ed. Michael J. Meyer, Lewiston, NY: The Edwin Mellen Press, 2000, 375–402.

7. It is such a well known taunt that when Jesse Ventura, the professional wrestler, became governor of Minnesota, many shops sold tee shirts reading, "My governor can beat your governor."

8. Steinbeck had a predilection and penchant for arcane and antique language. John Steinbeck IV tells of his father inviting the boys to picnic and "sit on the ground and tell sad stories of the deaths of kings" (110).

WORKS CITED

Benson, Jackson J. *The True Adventures of John Steinbeck, Writer*. New York: Viking, 1984.

French, Warren. *John Steinbeck*. New Haven, CT: Twayne, 1961, 53–61.

Gladstein, Mimi R. "*America and Americans*: The Arthurian Consummation," *After 'The Grapes of Wrath': Essays on John Steinbeck in Honor of Tetsumaro Hayashi*, Eds. Donald V. Coers, Paul D. Ruffin, Robert J. DeMott. Athens: Ohio University Press, 1995, 228–37.

———. "Friendly Fire: Steinbeck's *East of Eden*," *The Betrayal of Brotherhood in the Work of John Steinbeck*, ed. Michael J. Meyer, Lewiston, NY: The Edwin Mellen Press, 2000, 375–402.

Kinney, Arthur F. "The Arthurian Cycle in *Tortilla Flat*," *Steinbeck: A Collection of Critical Essays*, ed. Robert Murray Davis, Englewood Cliff, NJ: Prentice-Hall, 1972, 36–46.

Steinbeck, John. *Cannery Row*. New York: Penguin, 1945.

———. *East of Eden*. New York: Penguin, 1952.

———. *The Grapes of Wrath*. New York: Penguin, 1939.

———. *Journal of a Novel*. New York: Bantam, 1970.

———. *The Long Valley*. New York: Penguin, 1938.

———. *The Pastures of Heaven*. New York: Penguin, 1932.

Steinbeck, John, IV. "Adam's Wound," *The Betrayal of Brotherhood in the Work of John Steinbeck*, ed. Michael J. Meyer, Lewiston, NY: The Edwin Mellen Press, 2000, 99–110.

7

Lonely Ladies and Landscapes

A Comparison of John Steinbeck's "The White Quail" and Eudora Welty's "A Curtain of Green"

Charlotte Cook Hadella
Southern Oregon University

From the beginning of her literary career to the end, Eudora Welty concerned herself with the status and images of women in small-town America while avoiding the abrasive discourse against the patriarchy which often accompanies feminist critiques of such communities. Nevertheless, Welty did not overlook the gender-specific difficulties for women in rural society. Likewise, John Steinbeck, particularly in his early short stories, also featured women such as Elisa Allen in "The Chrysanthemums," Jelka in "The Murder," and Amy Hawkins in "Johnny Bear" who seek personal fulfillment beyond the boundaries of their sanctioned spheres. In early story collections by each author—Steinbeck's *The Long Valley*, published in 1938, and Welty's *A Curtain of Green*, published in 1941—a number of female characters are lonely, repressed, and in some cases depraved because of the patriarchal forces which mold their personalities and limit their arenas of action.[1]

In these story collections, appearing within a few years of each other, we encounter women who are unfulfilled in their roles as housewives—Elisa Allen in Steinbeck's "The Chrysanthemums" and Livvi in Welty's story "Livvi," for example. Yet the conflict resolution for these two stories reveals obvious contrasts: Elisa cries "weakly—like an old woman" (Steinbeck 18), while Livvi dances into the "bursting light of spring" (Welty 239). Stories about marital infidelity highlight similar contrasts: Jelka, in Steinbeck's "The Murder," conforms to obedient servitude after being beaten by her husband, while Ruby Fisher, in Welty's "A Piece of News," never admits her indiscretions. As Peter Schmidt points out in *The Heart of the Story*, Ruby's husband, Clyde, "refuses to act out the role of the conventional angry husband. Instead, he parodies it in a way that seems to be his unarticulated recognition of Ruby's right to have a double life not defined solely by her marriage to him" (36). In this story and others, Welty emphasizes the power of women to transcend socially constructed norms.

Although Steinbeck resisted the oversimplification of the cause/effect relationship between unfulfilled womanhood and the power of the patriarchy, his exploration of this theme generally blames patriarchal constructs of idealized womanhood for limiting and entrapping women. His short story "The White Quail," the subject of extensive critical commentary, crystallizes Steinbeck's treatment of this theme (Hadella 65–69). On the other hand, instead of pointing fingers, laying blame, so to speak, Welty weaves a complex system of symbols and imagery to illustrate how both men and women often conspire unconsciously to coerce a female member of the community into conformity. In "A Curtain of Green," the title story of Welty's first anthology (originally published in the *Southern Review* in 1939), a woman's garden clearly symbolizes both sociological and psychological entrapment. Welty, however, complicates the symbology, turning the garden imagery back upon itself, until it evolves into a mechanism for personal expression, rebellion, and release rather than conformity and confinement. This impulse to push the garden metaphor beyond either a replication or a refutation of the Eden myth as it is employed by Steinbeck (Owens 100) characterizes a key difference between Steinbeck's depiction of women in early to mid-twentieth century America and Welty's representation of women during that same time period. Close readings of "The White Quail" and "A Curtain of Green" bring this contrast into sharp focus.

From an omniscient narrative voice, the opening of "The White Quail" establishes the garden as a central symbol of the story. By the end of paragraph three, the narrative voice has fused with Mary Teller's voice and the controlling image of the garden has fused with Mary as well. In a mock dialectical questioning of herself about finding a husband, Mary says, "She didn't think so much, 'Would this man like such a garden?' but, 'Would the garden like a such a man?'

For the garden was herself, and after all she had to marry some one she liked" (22)

That Mary likes her prospective husband is not positively established in the first section of the story, however. The fourth paragraph begins with "When she met Harry Teller, the garden seemed to like him" (22). And then she remembers that she "let him kiss her," but when he became too ardent and expressed his lust with "You make me kind of hungry" (and one naturally goes to a garden for food when hungry), she became annoyed and "sent him home" (23). Mary's confusion about the nature of commitment that marriage requires is evident from the beginning of the story. Her only concept of commitment is of her commitment to herself as an individual apart from everyone and everything. At one with her perfect, sterile garden, Mary is unable to participate in a union with another person. Marriage is simply a means to an end for her, and that end is total isolation.

Thus Steinbeck presents Mary Teller in "The White Quail" as a woman whose perceptions are warped. Marilyn Mitchell, commenting on the opening paragraphs of the story, notes: "Steinbeck introduces the reader to the narrow world of Mary Teller's garden through a dormer window composed of leaded, diamond-shaped panes. The convex curvature of the window and the fragmentation of its space indicate that the vision of the person within, Mary Teller, is distorted" (28). Later in the story, Steinbeck employs this same technique to emphasize Mary's distorted perception of her marriage by reversing her position and having her outside in her garden looking into her living room and imagining that she sees herself sitting there with her husband. The scene, to her, is "like a picture, like a set of a play that was about to start" (27).

A number of critics have concluded that Mary's perceptions are warped and she is only deceiving herself to think that she will create something that "won't ever change" (24), whether it be a garden or a marriage. Louis Owens views Mary's garden "as a barrier between herself and all contact with the world outside . . . an attempt to construct an unfallen Eden in a fallen world, a neurotic projection of Mary's self" (113). Arthur Simpson, in discussing Mary's garden as a form of artistic withdrawal, says that it represents "static perfection" (12). And Brian Barbour comments that although a garden basically symbolizes fertility, Steinbeck uses it ironically "to deny change . . . and as a manifestation of Mary's sexual inhibition. . . . She keeps her garden, as she keeps herself, untrammeled" (117).

Yet Steinbeck does not hold Mary totally responsible for the sterile, static condition of her life and her marriage. In Part II of the "The White Quail," Harry becomes a willing partner in the illusive quest for a perfect Eden, a quest that destroys the couple's chances for a rewarding relationship. His admiration as she supervises the creation of the garden pleases Mary so much that she extends the following invitation: "You can plant some of the things you like in the garden, if you want" (23). Harry declines immediately what, in the context of the story's symbolism, is his only opportunity to consummate the marriage. And Mary, of course, "loved him for that" (24). But once her garden is completed just the way she wants it, with no contributions from Harry except his awe, Mary expresses a moment of misgiving when she says, "In a way I'm sad that it's done," which is followed by, "But mostly I'm glad. We won't ever change it, will we Harry? If a bush dies, we'll put another one just like it in the same place" (24). Mary's appointment of Harry as a keeper of the perfect Eden indicates her perception of his willingness to preserve the garden, forever untouched, unchanged—in other words, his willingness to preserve her chastity.

Stanley Renner, who describes Mary Teller as "ethereal, unearthly, fleshless," contends that the devotion she inspires from Harry is "suggestive of divine adoration rather than earthly love" ("Birds of a Feather" 37). Renner also acknowledges that Harry is a partner in Mary's self-idealization which is "set in the larger *cultural* idealization of womanhood itself" (36). Harry's comments at the end of Part II certainly support his role as worshipper of purity. He admits his fear of violating Mary (the garden) and he calls her "untouchable" (25). She responds with, "You let me do it. You made it my garden" (25). Renner observes that in "the pointless heart-shaped pool" which is the centerpiece of the garden, "Steinbeck has deftly symbolized the romantic ideal that lies at the heart of it all, a spiritualized, sexless, and thus, in several senses, pointless love" ("Sexual Idealism" 79).

Part II of the story features the description of the couple killing slugs and snails together in the garden, the introduction of the threatening cat, and Mary's speech proclaiming her fuchsias as a fortress from the "rough and tangle" world that wants to get into her garden (26). Critics agree that Harry's sexual needs are identified with the stalking cat which is mentioned in Part III, preparing the reader for the information in Part IV that Mary always locked her bedroom door and that Harry always tried the door silently" (30). Mary muses that it "seemed to make him ashamed when he turned the knob and found the door locked," but her response is to turn out the light in her bedroom and look out the window "at her garden in the half moonlight" (30). In this way, Steinbeck shows Mary retreating further into her unnatural world of illusory perception as Harry becomes less able to suppress his natural sexual urges.

Though Renner is correct in noting that the final two sections of the story "move toward a striking climax that dramatizes the explosive potential of the unconscious stresses building up in the marriage" ("Sexual Idealism" 83, 85), his contentions that Harry kills the quail unintentionally, and that this act shows Harry finally succumbing to his sexual urges in spite of Mary's protests, seem contradictory. It is more logical to assume that in a world as symbolically contrived as the world of the Teller's marriage, Steinbeck allows Harry to kill the white quail intentionally. Harry's violence against the symbol of Mary's chastity, an essence boiled down to utter purity (33), is a symbolic action by a character who is incapable of real action. It is also important to note that the cat does not even enter the picture in this scene. Mary's hysterical reaction may have scared him away from her garden forever; or Harry may simply have become the cat, symbolically.

Steinbeck includes a subtle detail in Part V of the story to underline Mary's ability to dominate Harry so thoroughly that he is only capable of symbolic violence. Just after she sees the white quail, Mary experiences a series of memories that she associates with the kind of pleasure that she felt at that moment. One of those memories is simply a statement someone once made about her—"She's like a gentian, so quite"—a statement which filled her with "an ecstasy" like the ecstasy in seeing the white quail (33). A gentian is a medicinal plant that destroys bacteria, and Mary, like a gentian, has sterilized her marriage completely, so completely that Harry is incapable of contaminating it even if he refuses to poison the cat.

The narrative shift from Mary's point of view to Harry's point of view at the end of the story emphasizes the total lack of understanding between man and wife. She cannot perceive of the despair that causes him to kill the quail. But the fact that the cat does not even appear in this scene indicates that Harry's violence against the quail and his remorse afterward are not simply eruptions of violent sexual urges but expressions of the altered environment of the marriage. Harry has become the cat, the Old Harry in Mary's Eden, the sexual threat, the potential "fall" that cannot be exorcised; but on a realistic level,

he and Mary cannot interact as marriage partners unless he resorts to
violence and forcefully invades her cloistral chamber.

Steinbeck suggests that self-induced isolation results from concepts
of womanhood espoused by an American society which quests for an
illusory Eden. He also demonstrates that such sterile self-repression
affects not only the females, but inspires violent reactions from the
men who attempt to interact with them. Harry never confronts Mary
openly with his hostility; instead he deliberately kills the white quail
that she begs him to rescue, and then he cries aloud to an empty
room," Oh, Lord, I'm so lonely!" (37). Although the "The White
Quail" does not present a particularly sympathetic view of the central
female character, the story clearly implies that the disunity in the marriage can be blamed on male idealization of female perfection.

A sense of isolation and loneliness also dominates Welty's story
"A Curtain of Green," but in this story, the wife longs for the male/
female union. Unfortunately, such a union is impossible because the
husband is deceased. Welty opens the story with this fact: Mrs. Larkin, since the day that her husband was killed by a falling chinaberry
tree, has "never once been seen anywhere else" but her garden (107).
Welty writes:

> Within its border of hedge, high like a wall, and visible only from the
> upstairs windows of the neighbors, this slanting, tangled garden, more
> and more overabundant and confusing, must have become so familiar
> to Mrs. Larkin that quite possibly by now she was unable to conceive of
> any other place. (107)

The widow's link to humanity seems to have been severed with
the death of her husband. Mr. Larkin, for whose father the town of
Larkin's Hill had been named, had obviously been a respected citizen,
and the townspeople had extended that respect to his wife as well.
The women of the town, we are told, "had called upon the widow
with decent frequency" (108). However, when Mrs. Larkin does not
respond as they wish, they withdraw, leaving her alone, only thinking of her when they "looked down from their bedroom windows as
they brushed studiously at their hair in the morning" (108). Stressing
the extremity of the rift between Mrs. Larkin and the other women of
Larkin's Hill, Welty notes that from their windows, "[t]hey found her
place in the garden, as they might have run their fingers toward a city
on a map of a foreign country, located her from their distance almost
in curiosity, and then forgot her" (108). As Peter Schmidt points out,

the world of the deceased husband "belongs to the front of the house,
the world of Larkin's Hill, whereas the only area in which his wife can
imagine living is *behind* the house, slanting away almost obscured
from view on the 'other' or 'back' side of the hill on which the town
is founded. Mrs. Larkin thus cultivates a secret life on the other side
of the town's public space, a subversive doubling and disfiguring that
expresses both energy and despair, entrapping her even as it provides
a form of release" (26).

Mrs. Larkin has obviously rejected the traditional role reserved for
her—the passive, seemingly trivial existence of her female neighbors
who appear "in the windows of their houses, fanning and sighing,
waiting for the rain" (107). On the day that the events of the story
take place, as the women watch Mrs. Larkin,

> the intense light like a tweezers picked out her clumsy, small figure in its
> old pair of men's overalls rolled up at the sleeves and trousers, separated
> it from the thick leaves, and made it look strange and yellow as she
> worked with a hoe—over-vigorous, disreputable, and heedless. (107)

The extravagant recklessness of Mrs. Larkin's garden, in fact, is what
separates her from the other women in the town whose lives are
ordered by tree-lined streets, rows of flower gardens, and window
frames. Rebelling against such monotony, "Mrs. Larkin rarely cut, sep-
arated, tied back [her plants]. . . . To a certain extent, she seemed not
to seek for order, but to allow an over-flowering, as if she consciously
ventured forever a little farther, a little deeper, into her life in the
garden" (108). Welty also stresses details of appearance and behavior
to emphasize that Mrs. Larkin is becoming more and more like her
garden and less like other women of the town: her hair is "streaming
and tangled"; she wanders about "uncertainly, deep among the plants
and wet with their dew" (107).

Referring to Welty's use of landscape in *Losing Battles*, Lucinda
MacKethan makes an observation which also applies to many of
Welty's stories, particularly to a "A Curtain of Green": "By focusing
on the natural world, then blending it with emotions of her characters through similes, [Welty] puts character and place together in
dynamic relationship" (189). A dynamic relationship obviously exists
between Mrs. Larkin and her garden, and the overriding characteristic
of that relationship is tension.

Noting that the "rich blackness of the soil" and the "extreme fertility" of the garden "formed at once a preoccupation and a challenge to

Mrs. Larkin" (108), Welty juxtaposes the abundance of the landscape against the apparent emptiness of Mrs. Larkin's family and community life. As for the other women of the town the only "place" to which Welty ever attaches them is a bedroom window: we never see them in a natural setting. The contrast between the "setting" of these women's lives and the "setting" of Mrs. Larkin's life intensifies the isolation of all of the women in the story and points to the barrenness of the lives of women in Larkin's Hill. This lack of meaningful activity, Carol Manning points out, leads to pettiness and inhumanity (54). Also contributing to the tension of the story is the fact that the rain, which usually came every afternoon by two o'clock, has not yet arrived. Even the women who only watch Mrs. Larkin and do not vigorously pursue gardening themselves are "waiting for the rain" (107).

What Welty illustrates with her description of the women's activities in "A Curtain of Green" is a pattern of ordering one's universe which Mackethan notes about Welty's fictional world in general: "Man, seeking his own identity, 'attaches' himself to a place because it offers a concrete mechanism through which he can order and hold onto the beliefs that give meaning to his life" (182). With Mrs. Larkin, however, we have a character attaching herself to a place of confusion and disorder and working energetically, obsessively, to promote even more confusion. Yet, the action itself has become the ordering device for Mrs. Larkin's universe. That the woman's frantic activities are a ritual to ease her sense of loss is clearly established early in the story. So, too, is the summer rain regarded ritualistically, as "a regular thing, [which] would come about two o'clock in the afternoon" (107). But on the day that the events of the story occur, two conditions arise which signal a disruption of the ritual: the rains have not come by late afternoon; and Mrs. Larkin has finally come to "one of the last patches of uncultivated ground" which she is clearing for some new shrubs (109). Clearly, Mrs. Larkin is approaching a point of crisis or catharsis: her gardening has provided her with a "curtain" of forgetfulness, but now she is running out of "uncultivated ground."

This subtle detail provides the operational metaphor for the story: with no new ground toward which to direct her energy, Mrs. Larkin will have to return to some area of the garden that she has already cultivated; there, she will have to nurture what already exists, or destroy the product of past efforts and begin all over again. As long as she has new ground to cultivate, she does not have to concern herself with past labors—does not have to deal with memory. She can simply move forward or in circles, drawing a curtain of green behind her. But, on the day that she reaches the last patch of uncultivated earth, "memory tightened about her easily, without any prelude or warning or even despair" (109). She sees "the fragrant chinaberry tree, suddenly tilting, dark and slow like a cloud, leaning down to her husband" (109). She recalls the absolute incredibility of not being able to control the events occurring before her eyes. When the flashback ends, Mrs. Larkin notices the stillness of her garden—the stasis of her world. The wind has ceased; birds have hushed: "The sun seemed clamped to the side of the sky. Everything had stopped once again, the stillness had mesmerized the stems of the plants, and the leaves went suddenly into thickness" (109).

To break the stillness, Mrs. Larkin calls angrily to Jamey, the black boy whom she occasionally hires to work in the garden. Suddenly, irrationally, she is infuriated by Jamey's "look of docility" (110), and what happens next is crucial to understanding the story: Mrs. Larkin moves toward Jamey with her hoe, notices that "he was lost in some impossible dream of his own" (110), and raises her hoe above his head as if to strike. Questions about life and death flash through her consciousness: "Was it not possible to compensate? To punish? To protest?" (111). The answer to her questions arrives in the form of rain, the natural occurrence which has come in its own time. Realizing that humans have no control over accidents of nature—a tree falling in the yard, the rain coming at dusk instead of at two o'clock—Mrs. Larkin lowers her hoe. Human beings, she concedes, cannot control nature, cannot even make sense sometimes of the events of their lives: but they can control their own actions. Standing close to Jamey, she "listened to the rain falling. It was so gentle. It was so full—the sound of the end of waiting" (111).

Ironically, Mrs. Larkin reaches the understanding toward which she has been ceaselessly striving by realizing that there is no rational explanation for the tragedy in her life, the separation from a husband with whom she passionately desires a reunion. "It has come, she thought senselessly, her head lifting and her eyes looking without understanding at the sky which had begun to move, to fold nearer in softening, dissolving clouds" (111). Once the grieving widow rejects the ratiocination which has paralyzed her since her husband's death, her world begins to move again. She looks forward to "the loud and gentle night of rain. . . . The day's work would be over in the garden. She would lie in bed, her arms tired at her sides and in motionless peace: against that which was inexhaustible, there was no defense" (111). Then Mrs. Larkin faints, and as she lies there among her flowers with the rain falling on woman and garden alike, Jamey looks at her "unknowing face, white and rested under its bombardment" (112); then, before running away, he calls to her until she stirs.

Critics have not dealt very thoroughly with the perplexing conclusion to "A Curtain of Green." Ruth M. Vande Kieft says the only relief from pain with which a reader leaves this story comes from "the perception of some kind of order in the work itself and of truth seen and faced, and the catharsis of pity and fear" (32). Michael Kreyling believes that the woman's unconsciousness is her passage from the modernist world of self-conscious isolation into a natural, "unseen world" where "the lost intangibles of vital human existence would once again appear as 'living realities'" (51). But since the story ends with Mrs. Larkin in a state of semi-consciousness and the last recorded impression of her stresses her "unknowing face," it seems unreasonable to conclude that she has had any revelation beyond the acceptance of her "unknowingness." Moreover, Welty reminds us that even if Mrs. Larkin learns to deal with her husband's death, she still faces a hostile, or at best, indifferent human community as represented by the other women of Larkin's Hill.

Her isolation, therefore, is neither totally self-imposed nor entirely solipsistic. The author inserts this reminder at the very end of the story by having Jamey recall that all the while Mrs. Larkin had been standing over him he had heard "the oblivious crash of the windows next door being shut when the rain started" (112). If Mrs. Larkin has succeeded in becoming "one of her own cultivations" (Kreyling 51) by merging with the natural world, then the community which promptly shuts itself away from natural phenomena will surely continue to close itself against an "over-vigorous, disreputable, and heedless" woman (107). Louis Rubin notes that human communities in Welty's fictions "are founded on the agreement . . . not to admit to the existence of chaos and violence that cannot be controlled, explained, scaled down to manageable proportion" (111). It is quite possible, then, that Mrs. Larkin's realizations will only further isolate her from human society.

By bringing our attention back to the women in the windows of Larkin's Hill, Welty demonstrates a concern for the whole female community and not just a concern for Mrs. Larkin alone. Not directly, but subliminally, Welty shows us the sad results of a patriarchal cultural bias which deprives women of meaningful work and productive outlets for creative expression. Instead, the acceptable feminine sphere in the small Southern town is the garden club meeting (not the garden) in which the members discuss "what constitute[s] an appropriate vista, or an effect of restfulness, or even harmony of color" (108), or the dressing table, where women may sit and brush "studiously at their hair" (108). When Mrs. Larkin does regain consciousness, she may retain her sense of relief over accepting her husband's death as an irrational occurrence that she can never understand. Whether she can penetrate her garden wall, whether she can find meaning for her own life as a woman without a husband around which to order her existence, Welty leaves unanswered. At the end of "A Curtain of Green," Mrs. Larkin's choices as a woman in Larkin's Hill seem quite limited: to become like her neighbors, to take her seat behind a window, she will have to cease being a woman with the vitality, the passion, and penchant for prolific growth to which her garden is testimony. Welty does not push the narrative to this either/or conclusion.

Welty's quiet open-endedness in the final scene of "A Curtain of Green" contrasts starkly with Steinbeck's direct declaration of outcomes. Clearly, Mary Teller's self absorption in "The White Quail" is complete: she delivers her last spoken words of the story from behind her locked bedroom door. Her husband's final words are "Oh, Lord, I'm so lonely!" (37). Steinbeck's story lays out a dialectic discourse of cause and effect: the obsessive female gardener seeks stasis, perfection, self absorption; she takes societal expectations of idealized womanhood to a neurotic extreme. Her male counterpart commits symbolic murder out of anger and frustration. On the other hand, Welty's obsessive gardener seeks growth and change, a shattering of societal constructs, and release from self-absorption. She resists performing an act of murder to balance out the random cruelty of the universe, a randomness that has left her widowed, lonely, and frustrated.

The comparison of these two stories and their varied implementation of the "woman as garden" motif points to the influence of gender perspectives. Though neither author delivers conclusive conflict resolutions, Steinbeck more clearly than Welty blames the male's obsession with female purity for the loneliness and neurosis of humankind. The final words in "The White Quail" are spoken by the man who has co-created his own despair as he looks through his living room window at the perfect garden. Whereas Mary Teller aims to keep out the rough and tangled world, which includes a consummated marriage, Welty's

Mrs. Larkin creates a rough and tangled landscape in her effort to come to terms with the destruction of her marital union. Steinbeck's exploration of the male perspective clearly accounts for major differences between the two authors' social commentary: while "A Curtain of Green" emphasizes a process of healing by focusing on human *need*, "The White Quail" focuses on *blame*.

NOTE

1. My discussion of "The White Quail" as it appears in this current essay reiterates my original reading of that story as it appeared in "Steinbeck's Cloistered Women."

WORKS CITED

Barbour, Brian. "Steinbeck as a Short Story Writer." *A Study Guide to Steinbeck's "The Long Valley."* Ed. Tetsumuro Hayashi. Ann Arbor, MI: Pierian Press, 1976.

Hadella, Charlotte. "Steinbeck's Cloistered Women." *The Steinbeck Question.* Ed. Donald R Noble. Troy, New York: Whitson Publishing Company, 1993.

Kreyling, Michael. "Modernism in Welty's *A Curtain of Green and Other Stories.*" *Southern Quarterly* 20 4 (Summer 1982): 40–53.

MacKethan, Lucinda Hardwick. *The Dream of Arcady: Place and Time in Southern Literature.* Baton Rouge: Louisiana State UP, 1980.

Mannin, Carol S. *With Ears Opening Like Morning Glories: Eudora Welty and the Love of Story Telling.* Westport, CT: Greenword Press, 1985.

Mitchell, Marilyn. "Steinbeck's Strong Women: Feminine Identity in the Short Stories." *Steinbeck's Women: Essays in Criticism.* Ed. Tetsumuro Hayashi. Muncie, IN: Ball State University Press, 1979.

Owens, Louis. *John Steinbeck's Re-Vision of America.* Athens: University of Georgia Press, 1985.

Renner, Stanley. "Mary Teller and Sue Bridehead: Birds of a Feather in "The White Quail" and *Jude the Obscure.*" *Steinbeck Quarterly* 18 (1985).

———. "Sexual Idealism and Violence in "The White Quail." *Steinbeck Quarterly* 17 (1984).

Schmidt, Peter. *The Heart of the Story: Eudora Welty's Short Fiction.* Jackson: University of Mississippi Press, 1991.

Simpson, Arthur. "'The White Quail': A Portrait of an Artist." *A Study Guide to Steinbeck's "The Long Valley."* Ed. Tetsumuro Hayashi. Ann Arbor, MI: Pierian Press, 1976.

Steinbeck, John. *The Long Valley*. New York: Viking Press, 1986. All page numbers for the parenthetical citations of Steinbeck's stories discussed here refer to this edition.

Vande Kieft, Ruth M. "Eudora Welty: The Question of Meaning." *Southern Quarterly* 20.4 (Summer 1982): 28–39.

Welty, Eudora. *The Collected Stories of Eudory Welty*. New York: Harcourt Brace Jovanovich, 1980. All page numbers for the parenthetical citations of Welty's stories discussed here refer to this edition.

Part 4

STEINBECK, THE AMERICAN IDEAL, POLITICS, AND WAR

Regardless of the degree to which *The Winter of Our Discontent* is artistically satisfactory—and I would suggest by my formalistic analysis that it is more artistically coherent than is generally acknowledged—it is a unique and unlikely to be emulated investigation of the American ideal under threat.

—Stephen L. Tanner

8

Steinbeck's *The Winter of Our Discontent* and the American Ideal

Stephen L. Tanner
Brigham Young University

In speaking of an American ideal, I have particularly in mind these definitions of the word *ideal*: existing as an archetypal idea, a mental image or conception, a standard of excellence. My contention is that John Steinbeck was alone among the major novelists of his time in concerning himself with America as an idea, as a distinct and coherent entity. This entity is the focus of his last three books: *The Winter of Our Discontent* (1961), *Travels with Charley* (1962), and *America and Americans* (1966). Jackson Benson refers to them as Steinbeck's "moral trilogy" (*True Adventures* 968). They are more accurately described as his "America trilogy." The subtitle of *Travels with Charley*, "In Search of America," could serve equally well for the other two. Using three genres—novel, travel narrative, and essay—Steinbeck attempted to ascertain the nature of America and examine its current moral health. The endeavor was both admirable and misguided. It was admirable in its sincerity, its sympathetic probing, and its frankness of critical perception. There is considerable benefit in observing a humane author like Steinbeck, in his mature years, as he focuses a loving but stringent eye on his own nation. But the endeavor was also misguided. The magnitude and complexity of the task dictated that it could only partially be realized. America as idea or fact defies formulation and encapsulation. Moreover, the actuality of an American entity, a distinct

American character, is debatable and nowadays aggressively denied. There may also have been a problem in his being so self-consciously "in search of America." Deliberate searching does not always result in good art. Artistic insight often comes by instinct—uninvited, unforced, and without conscious direction. In the case of *The Winter of Our Discontent*, self-conscious preoccupation with the American ideal seems to have interfered with the artistry. For many readers, proposition outstrips presentation.

Why was Steinbeck so preoccupied with the American ideal in his final trilogy? According to Louis Owens, his entire life had been a search for America: "Steinbeck's fiction constitutes the most ambitious and thorough examination of the idea of America yet produced by any writer. It is a life's work focused on the singular attempt to understand for America the great myth upon which the nation was founded" (208). Many would agree, but regardless of how long or deliberate that search had been during his lifetime, it became an obvious and explicit absorption during his final decade. He was not a philosopher, but he was always a man of ideas, and his urgent need to bring his ideas to the attention of others was the main impulse for his writing. At the end of the fifties, he had enough ideas about his country to power three very different kinds of books. *Travels* explores the geography of America, its external life. The essays of *America and Americans* are, in the words of its editors, "jeremiads, exhorting America to take heed" (314). *Winter* is a fictional embodiment of the American ideal under threat from an insidious immorality. He described this threat in a letter to a friend in September 1959: "Immorality is what is destroying us, public immorality. The failure of man toward men, the selfishness that puts making a buck more important than the common weal" (*True Adventures* 858). Two months later, he wrote to Adlai Stevenson, "We can stand anything God or Nature can throw at us save only plenty. If I wanted to destroy a nation, I would give it too much and I would have it on its knees, miserable, greedy and sick" (*A Life in Letters* 652). This frustration with what he perceived as a moral torpor and spiritual laxity in America appears often in his letters of the late fifties and early sixties.

Among the causes of this frustration was his extensive travel abroad during the late fifties. This distance allowed him to see his own country with new, critical eyes. His experience was much like Hawthorne's a century earlier. Hawthorne also went abroad and became acutely conscious of the slow disintegration in competitive America of the bases on which earlier moral values had depended. He wrote to his publisher, "The United States are fit for many excellent purposes, but they are certainly not fit to live in" (Matthiessen 361). Steinbeck similarly complained of the difficulties of living and rearing a family in America: "It is very hard to raise boys to love and respect virtue and learning when the tools of success are chicanery, treachery, self-interest, laziness and cynicism or when charity is deductible, the courts venal, the highest public official placid, vain, slothful and illiterate" (Steinbeck to Dag Hammarskjöld, *A Life in Letters* 653). John Timmerman suggests that Steinbeck's awareness of a moral darkening in contemporary America was heightened by his extensive research on King Arthur and the age of Camelot while he was living in England. The contrasts and parallels intrigued him (256–57).

Steinbeck's fascination with the idea of America derived partly from his political inclinations. He was a lifetime Democrat and was genuinely interested in politics and national ideals. He established friendships with political figures such as Adlai Stevenson and enjoyed talking about the concept of America. As cynical as he might seem in his comments on particular political situations and personalities, he had an abiding faith in and love for the mythic concept of America as a land of freedom, opportunity, and moral rectitude. He found much in American character and achievement to admire. He never imbibed in the expatriate aloofness of other American writers of his generation. Elaine Steinbeck said in 1993, "One of the first things I asked John when I first met him was, 'When Fitzgerald and Hemingway were abroad, why didn't you go?' And he said, 'I didn't have the price of a ticket.' And he said, 'I'm very glad now that I didn't because I stayed at home and wrote about my own people'" (Coers 240). His involvement in the nation's propaganda efforts during World War II only fortified his commitment to the idea of America and deepened his attachment to the patriotic myths and traditions on which that idea was founded.

He clearly believed in the existence of a distinct unit, entity, or ideal called America. "The motto of the United States, '*E Pluribus Unum*,' is a fact," he insisted. "Our land is of every kind geologically and climatically, and our people are of every kind also—of every race, of every ethnic category—and yet our land is one nation, and our people are Americans" (*America and Americans* 319). In *Travels*, he asserts that "The American identity is an exact and provable thing." Despite its obvious diversity, he maintains America is of a piece: "For all our enormous geographical range, for all of our sectionalism, for all of our interwoven breeds from every part of the ethnic world, we are a nation, a new breed. Americans are much more American than they are Northerners, Southerners, Westerners, or Easterners. . . . This is not patriotic whoop-de-do; it is carefully observed fact" (185–86). Americans are indeed individuals, he acknowledged, "each one different from the others, but gradually I began to feel that Americans exist, that they really do have generalized characteristics regardless of their states, their social and financial status, their education, their religious, and their political convictions" (215–16). Steinbeck's prefatory statement to *Winter* leaves no doubt that his purpose is to reveal something about America: "Reader's seeking to identify the fictional people and places here described would do better to inspect their own communities and search their own hearts, for this book is about a large part of America today." It is the American community, the American idea that interests him.

If, as Louis Owens contends, Steinbeck's is the most ambitious and thorough examination of the idea of America, it is also undoubtedly the last of its kind. His America trilogy immediately preceded a revolutionary shift of perspective regarding America, followed by the emergence of a revisionist American history. With the advent of poststructualism and its emphasis on difference and antifoundationalism, the notion of an American ideal, an American character, became a prime target for deconstruction in its various forms. A parade of trends and fashions in criticism, set in motion by French theory at the end of the sixties, has marched to the unifying tune of hostility toward the American ideal. Charges of racism, sexism, classism, imperialism, homophobia, hegemony, and mystification have been cloyingly leveled at the idea of America. Steinbeck's criticism of American capitalism may still be palatable, but, for many, the ideals on which it was based are not. The concept of America he sought to clarify and promote in his final years would, within a decade of his death, become the bête noire of academia.

I turn now to *The Winter of Our Discontent*. The cover of the first paperback edition describes the book as "the novel of an honest man's struggles with the seductive temptations of today's easy money and morals." In what follows, I wish to demonstrate the central role played by what might be called the American ideal in these struggles. The central conflict in the novel is the opposition between money and the American ideal. This statement may seem an oversimplification, but I intend to demonstrate its soundness.

The money side of the opposition is obvious. Plot, characterization, and even setting (e.g., the grocery store being next to the bank) are determined by money. Money is the dominant theme or leitmotif throughout the novel, which includes a litany of unethical money schemes: bribes, kickbacks, malfeasance, rigged quiz shows, loss leaders, graft, shady real estate deals, and general sharp dealing. From his children, Ethan repeatedly hears statements like these: "When are you going to be rich?" "I'm sick of being poor" (85). "I wish we had some money" (191). "Do you think I like to live without no motorbike? Must be twenty kids with motorbikes. And how you think it is if your family hasn't even got a car, leave alone no television" (82). Besides the frequent mention of money and money matters, Steinbeck uses two particular techniques to convey the pervasive acquisitiveness in contemporary American society. The first is to repeat clichés regarding money-making as a way of suggesting how ingrained and unexamined the acquisitive instinct is lodged in the American psyche. "Everybody's got a right to make a buck" (29). "A guy got to make a buck! Look out for number one!" (255). "Money gets money" (64, 125, 162). "And that is the money that makes money. It doesn't matter how you get it just as long as you get it and use it to make more" (66). "A reputation for money is almost as negotiable as money itself" (119). "There are the eaters and the eaten. That's a good rule to start with" (54). "You have to look after number one" (25, 222). "Just remember number one" (232). "Grab anything that goes by. It may not come around again." "Grab the gold ring for a free ride" (187). "Everybody does it" (29, 190). The very plot of the novel is based on the playful cliché that robbing a bank is the best way to get money fast. The sin of avarice in this society is trivialized. As Steinbeck observed in *America and Americans*, the real danger is not the miscreants but our attitude toward them: "Increasingly we lose our feeling of wrong" (396-97).

Steinbeck's second technique for conveying the depth of America's worship of money-getting is to use images of superstition and religious reverence. Love of money, he implies, has poisoned the innate human hunger for transcendence. Margie, with her aura of witchcraft and fortune-telling (fortune, in this case being rather exclusively money), bewitches the innocent Mary into superstitious expectations. Mary's deepest metaphysical longings, suggested by the Easter season, are contaminated by superstitious hope for money. A similar perversion of spiritual impulses is suggested when Mr. Baker's opening of the Bank vault is described as a religious ceremony in which "Father Baker genuflects and opens the safe and we all bow down to the Great God Currency" (150). Ethan describes the process this way: "They practically stood at attention as the clock hand crossed nine. There came a click and buzzing from the great steel safe door. Then Joey dialed the *mystic* numbers and turned the wheel that drew the bolts. The *holy of holies* swung stately open and Mr. Baker took the *salute* of the assembled money. I stood outside the rail like a humble *communicant* waiting for the *sacrament*" (221, italics added). As his use of these two techniques suggests, the immorality that alarmed Steinbeck in the fifties was spiritual as well and ethical; its damaging effects penetrated deeply into man's spiritual core.

A strength of the novel is Steinbeck's delineation of the insidious pressure American acquisitiveness exerts on even good and wise men. Ethan is well aware that money is no guarantee of happiness. When his wife suggests that it can be, he says, "It's a despairing unhappiness I'm afraid of, the panic money brings, the protectiveness and the envy" (129). When his wife says, "I don't see how a little money could spoil anything. Not a lot of money—just enough," he replies, "There is no such thing as just enough money. Only two measures: No Money and Not Enough Money" (128). While communing with the cans and bottles on the store shelves, he has this significant thought: "Money not only has no heart but no honor nor any memory" (66). Of course, honor and memory—specifically his family honor and history—are vitally important to him. But his knowledge of the dangers of money notwithstanding, he succumbs to its temptations all the same. At one point he tries to justify himself by thinking his crime "was not a crime against men, only against money. No one would get hurt. Money is insured." (241). The complex ways in which money seems requisite to the happiness of his family and to his own self-respect overwhelm him.

The other side of the novel's central conflict is what I have called the American ideal. This term designates the complex of American history, literature, tradition, myths, and values that Steinbeck brings into play as a norm by which to highlight and judge the damaging effects of obsession with money. This pattern of references and allusions begins early in the novel. In the opening lines, Ethan quotes the traditional American folk song "Froggy Went a Courting" (5). And Ethan's name, of course, is itself part of the pattern. He and his son share the same name: Ethan Allen Hawley. His mother's family "came over on the *Mayflower*," and he feels he is related to Ethan Allen, a hero of the American Revolutionary War (10–11). Incidentally, the name is linked with a famous brand of traditional American furniture. He is a graduate of Harvard and his name is on the town's war memorial among the surviving heroes of World War II (48, 230). Also on the first page are references to Pilgrim Fathers, whaling ancestors, privateers, and the Continental Congress (5). Ethan stems from both the nation's Puritan roots and its enterprising early commercial roots, as represented by whaling. These two sides of his background remain in the reader's mind through the frequent references to his "New England Great Aunt Deborah" (42), referred to once as "little Plymouth Rock Aunt Deborah" (61), and to the Old Cap'n, his grandfather. The house he lives in was his great-grandfather's, "white-painted shiplap with a fanlight over the front door, and Adam decorations and a widow walk on the roof" (8). "They knew how to build in those days," Ethan remarks (8). The house is on Elm Street, a traditional American street name, and the elms are as old as the Early American houses (45) and are planted "on the original streets" (181). The town is New Baytown (perhaps suggesting Massachusetts Bay, one of the original American colonies), and it is "an old town, one of the first clear and defined whole towns in America" (43). Ethan's family has lived here "since the middle of the seventeen hundreds" (25). He represents "twenty generations of Hawleys and Allens" (191). These "patriotic and virtuous" ancestors had fought in the Revolutionary War and the War of 1812 (65).

Also within the first few pages is a slight, off-hand allusion that is nevertheless fraught with significance. As Ethan leaves for work, he says, "Farewell, oh ship of state" (8). The allusion is to Longfellow's "The Building of the Ship," a revered patriotic poem containing these lines:

> Thou, too, sail on, O Ship of State!
> Sail on, O UNION, strong and great!
> Humanity with all its fears,
> With all its hopes of future years,
> Is hanging breathless on thy fate!

This is an example of the sometimes subtle ways Steinbeck interjects the America ideal. Another example occurs a few pages later when

Ethan and his friend stop to look at "the old Bay Hotel, now being wrecked to make room for the new Woolworth. The yellow-painted bulldozer and the big crane that swung the wrecking ball were silent like waiting predators in the early morning" (12). Unobtrusively, this scene intimates the theme of tradition under threat from the commercial present. Louis Owens is correct in identifying Ethan as modern American Everyman and New Baytown as microcosmic America (199). The novel is centered on an implied contrast between impressive things of the past and the much diminished versions of the present.

The pattern of references associated with the American ideal includes quotations from Thomas Paine: "These are the times that try men's souls" (275); from Lincoln's Gettysburg Address: "We cannot dedicate, we cannot consecrate" (259); and from Patrick Henry: "I know not what course others may take, but as for me, give me liberty or give me death!" (81). In referring to America's past, Ethan says, "There were giants on the earth in those days" (81). The past Steinbeck wishes to set reverberating as a contrasting foil for the present could be epitomized by these words of John Adams in a letter to his wife, Abigail: he prays that "neither ambition, nor vanity, nor any base motive, or sordid passion" should draw us aside from "the line of duty and the dictates of our consciences. Let us have ambition enough to keep our simplicity, our frugality, and our integrity, and transmit these virtues as the fairest inheritance to our children" (McCullough 238). Ethan attempts to transmit such an inheritance to his son, telling him, "There are unchanging rules of conduct, of courtesy, of honesty, yes, even of energy" (191). This is the sort of American ideal Ethan himself is enticed away from.

Besides quotations, there are references to *Moby Dick* (8), Thoreau, Whitman, Emerson, Mark Twain, the speeches of Jefferson, Lincoln, Webster, and Henry Clay (35–36, 83, 306), the Declaration of Independence, the Bill of Rights, and the words on the Statue of Liberty (254–55). Such a pattern makes it particularly appropriate that the climax of the novel should come around the Fourth of July, America's most patriotic holiday. This holiday is blighted by the destruction of the American ideal, epitomized by Ethan's change into a money schemer and Allen's cheating on the "Why I Love America" contest. Similarly, Easter had been blighted by Mary's superstitious hope for money through Margie's fortune telling and by the pervasive worship of the Great God Currency. On Good Friday, as Biggers, the wholesale representative, instructs Ethan on the system of kickbacks and tells him "everybody does it," Ethan remarks, "It's a dark day." Biggers, blind to Ethan's real meaning, replies, "No, it's not. You got the shades pulled down" (29).

In addition to such references and allusions, Steinbeck incorporates the American ideal into the symbolic action of the novel. Specifically, the talisman and "the light" function as symbolic indicators of the American ideal. The talisman is a "mound of translucent stone" that is kept in a cabinet containing the family's heritage of small objects. Ethan had always considered the cabinet with its brass lock from colonial times as "the holy place of the *parenti*" or the lares and penates of his family. These terms refer to household gods or objects sacred to the family. The talisman is such an object, "a continuity thing that inflames and comforts and inspires from generation to generation." It is described as "living," "like flesh," and "always warm to the touch" (142–43). As child, boy, and man, Ethan had been allowed to touch it, "and its color and convolutions and texture changed as [his] needs changed" (143). It is associated with Aunt Deborah, who told him, "It means what you want it to mean" (228), and it is also linked with his daughter Ellen, who is even drawn in her sleep to caress it. Ethan wonders, "Did the stone bring her somehow close to me—to the Hawleys?" (145). When Ellen asks the same question he had asked his Aunt Deborah, "What's a talisman?" he tells her the same thing Aunt Deborah had told him: "Look it up in the dictionary" (296). The talisman is important to Ellen as it has been to Ethan: "she will have the strange authority of Aunt Deborah" (216); she is "the light-bearer" (311).

Although Steinbeck gives the talisman a certain magic, mystic, and ambiguous quality, it is clearly intended to represent the continuity of family heritage and values, which in turn represents a continuity of the American ideal. And that ideal Steinbeck links with an ancient light of honor and rectitude (260). At a critical point, Ethan traces "the serpent on the talisman and came back to the beginning, which was the end. That was an old light. . . . And that light had not gone out" (260).

Ethan's children represent the two opposing forces in the novel: money and the American ideal. Allen, at least at this stage of his life, is thoroughly absorbed in the get-rich-at-any cost mentality dominating his society. His father suggests that he is determined to destroy America by embracing dishonesty (190). When Ethan finds Allen before the mirror after the boy has dishonestly won honorable mention in the

"Why I Love America" contest, he sees that "he had painted on a narrow black mustache, had darkened his brows and raised the outer ends
to satanic tips"; he is smiling "a world-wise, cynical charm into the
mirror" (293). This is a caricature personification of the immorality
Steinbeck felt was undermining America. For Allen the great speeches
of the nation are "patriotic jazz" to be exploited for material gain (81).
For Ellen, on the other hand, they are great. Ellen is now the keeper of
the talisman and the light it represents. She goes to it to charge "her
battery" (276). It is she who slips it in her father's pocket, where he
finds it when he is reaching for a razor to slit his wrists. It saves him:
"I had to get back—had to return the talisman to its new owner. Else
another light might go out" (311). To keep the light of the American
ideal, and the enduring values he thought it embodied, burning was
a large concern in Steinbeck's final years. The dedication to the novel
indicates this: "To Beth, my sister, whose light burns clear." On July 1,
1960, as he was completing the book, he wrote to Pascal Covici , "At
worst it should amuse, at half-staff move to emotion and at best *illumi-
nate*. And I don't know whether this will do any of those things but its
intention is the third" (*A Life in Letters* 676–77, italics added).

What did Steinbeck mean by keeping the light burning? Near the
conclusion of the novel, Ethan recognizes that the old Cap'n's light
and Aunt Deborah's light still burned, and, ironically, Marullo's light
still burned. The Italian had been forced to learn the hard lessons of
American materialism, but he had never lost the idealism embodied
in the words on the Statue of Liberty and in the Declaration of Independence and the Bill of Rights, which he had once memorized
(311, 254–55). Ethan, whose ability to see his ancestors clearly had
been fading as he betrayed the ideals they represented, discovers, "My
light is out." And he realizes, "It's so much darker when a light goes
out than it would have been if it had never shone" (311). This same
fading of ancestral ideals is symbolized by the yellowed white plume
on the Knight Templar hat. His family "had been Masons since before
George Washington had been Grand Master" (149). Ethan now uses
the hat box in his bank-robbing plan. To keep the light burning means
to retain a sense of idealism, and for Steinbeck that meant a distinctively American brand of idealism. If one looks for the profit motive
in American life, one finds it on every hand; but that monochromatic
perspective blurs differences and obliterates principles. This statement
from *America and Americans* is an apt commentary on the action of
Winter: "Once Adlai Stevenson, speaking of a politician of particularly

rancid practices, said 'If he were a bad man, I wouldn't be so afraid of him. But this man has no principles. He doesn't know the difference.' Could this be our difficulty, that gradually we are losing our ability to tell the difference? The rules fall away in chunks and in the vacant places we have a generality: 'It's all right because everybody does it'" (394). This is when the light goes out. This is when we must turn to the talisman of the American ideal. Steinbeck does not simplistically reject commerce. It is one part of his American heritage: his whaling ancestors who profited as privateers during the Revolutionary War. That traditional American commerce had not entirely lost sight of principle. Symbolically this part is represented by the Old Cap'n and his narwhal cane, which at a critical time Ethan takes with him "for self-protection" (296). But ultimately it is the talisman and all that it represents that saves him.

Winter is generally not placed high in the Steinbeck canon. John Timmerman believes that, conceptually, the novel "represents a culmination in Steinbeck's development as a moralist, in which he asserts that the abolition of moral norms for action is ultimately an abolition of man." But although the theme is worthy, the book fails by "the inability of the artistic craft to match the moral concern." The moral intensity is clear but the artistry is uncertain and shadowy (263, 265). As a reviewer pointed out, it takes more than an incontrovertible thesis to make a good novel: the writer must fill the arteries of his characters with blood (McElrath 462). Jackson Benson draws this perceptive conclusion regarding what I have called Steinbeck's America trilogy: "The sadness of John Steinbeck, writer, during the last years of his life was that although he had the will to advance—a will that was almost superhuman in its determination—none of the solutions that he tried were very satisfactory" (*True Adventures* 759). Regardless of the degree to which *The Winter of Our Discontent* is artistically satisfactory—and I would suggest by my formalistic analysis that it is more artistically coherent than is generally acknowledged—it is a unique and unlikely to be emulated investigation of the American ideal under threat.

WORKS CITED

Benson, Jackson J. *The True Adventures of John Steinbeck, Writer*. New York: Penguin, 1984.

Coers, Donald V., Paul D. Ruffin, and Robert J. DeMott, eds. *After the Grapes of Wrath: Essays on John Steinbeck.* Athens: Ohio University Press, 1995.

McCullough, David. *John Adams.* New York: Simon and Schuster, 2001.

McElrath, Joseph R., Jesse Crisler, and Susan Shillinglaw, eds. *John Steinbeck: The Contemporary Reviews.* Cambridge: Cambridge University Press, 1996.

Matthiessen, F. O. *American Renaissance.* New York: Oxford UP, 1941.

Owens, Louis. *John Steinbeck's Re-Vision of America.* Athens: University of Georgia Press, 1985.

Steinbeck, Elaine and Robert Wallsten, eds. *Steinbeck: A Life in Letters.* New York: Viking, 1975.

Steinbeck, John. *America and Americans and Selected Nonfiction.* Eds. Susan Shillinglaw and Jackson J. Benson. New York: Viking, 2002.

———. *Travels with Charley: In Search of America.* New York: Viking, 1962.

———. *The Winter of Our Discontent.* New York: Viking, 1961.

Timmerman, John H. *John Steinbeck's Fiction: The Aesthetics of the Road Taken.* Norman: University Oklahoma Presss, 1986.

9

Art for Politics

The Political Dimension of Steinbeck's Works in Eastern Europe

Danica Cerce
University of Ljubljana, Slovenia

Just as it is impossible to neglect the political implications of literary masterpieces and concur with Nietzsche that the aesthetic is the only justification for the world, as he writes in *The Birth of Tragedy*, so it is wrong to believe, with Levine, that "all things are political," and on the basis of this theory, replace literary studies with cultural or political ones (378–79). However, during the communist era, a genuine work of art was worth at least as much as any major political act. By joining this concept of art for politics with the voices that defend the necessity of the text-oriented analysis, my essay aims to present the intrinsic connections between the critical reception of Steinbeck's works with a newly devised set of concepts regarding the creative potential of fictional worlds in communist Eastern Europe.

As the history of the discipline shows, literature and literary discourses have the potential to reinforce the structures of domination and suppression. Similarly, they have the capacity to "disrupt the exercise of power" and create alternative worlds (Levine 384). This is precisely what happened in Eastern Europe during the era following the communist takeover. Because of the utilitarian conception of what constitutes the literary and the assimilation of literature to ideology, works of art were manipulated by communist propaganda and inadvertently served as a political tool. Criticism became a radical

ideological revision of the canon; consequently, many important classical works disappeared from academic curricula, as Harold Bloom
points out. Among many other books that were consigned to oblivion
because of their potential to foster autonomous thinking and subvert
the oppressive regime was Steinbeck's *In Dubious Battle*, which nevertheless helped shatter the well-worn cliché of communism. Perhaps
nowhere more than in Ceausescu's Romania, intellectuals became
aware of the fact that "art is the only reliable access to reality, because
it is the only mode that incorporates and preserves imperfection,
rather than trying for coherence and uniformity," as Virgil Nemoianu
asserts in his *Theory of the Secondary* (158).

Under the dominance of Soviet political concepts and power, East
European countries all shared a long history of censorship, confis-
cation, intrusions by the police, arrest, and imprisonment. In this
climate, antagonistic to speculative thought and governed by the
philosophical and ideological imperatives announced by the regime,
there was no room for critical thinking and creative imagination.
The only permissible thinking was that which was in accord with
the utopian communist model of social improvement. The tendency
to assign a special role to discourses that empowered the idealistic
prejudices of popular Marxism led critics to pursue the social aspects
and progressive elements in literary works. For them, literature was
merely another ideological discourse, an important locus for debat-
ing socio-political action. The production and reading of literary texts
were strictly controlled by a state. Needless to say, considering these
conditions, the few voices defending the relevance of aesthetics in
interpreting literature were outnumbered by those who embraced the
need for politically and ideologically committed reading. Because of
its potentially dangerous implications, every book had to undergo a
radical ideological revision before it was allowed to be published.

It goes without saying that the politicization of the act of interpretation and the rejection of the formalist approach preferred by aes-
theticians could hardly offer valuable insights into literary texts, nor
properly present a writer's oeuvre. Read simplistically and tenden-
tiously, almost any text can become a political tool, but it is a gross
simplification to see Steinbeck's *In Dubious Battle* as a social solution
capable of subverting capitalism (Suklje), or consider *Of Mice and
Men* in the first place a "remarkable social protest against the existing agricultural labor situation in California," as Janko Moder claims
in his 1983 assessment of the novel. Similarly, can *Tortilla Flat* be

read as a "hymn to chivalric ideals such as friendship, loyalty and simplicity," as Dusan Mevlja writes in 1953? Or can *East of Eden* be evaluated in the light of communist ideals, as it is in Joze Turk's 1980 accompanying study to the fourth Slovene translation of the novel? These examples, all representative of Slovene critical thought, clearly indicate that Steinbeck was expected to consistently produce works in which he would attack the capitalist world. By neglecting the richness and heterogeneity of Steinbeck's works, they provided for the fundamentally paradoxical position of the writer and his works in Slovene culture. In other countries, too, Steinbeck was treated unjustly: not only because the "ideological burden was a necessity," but also because some critics "consciously compromised their beliefs" to get a book to the readers (Kopecký 88).

The translation of *The Grapes of Wrath* as early as 1941 in Czechoslovakia, 1943 in Slovenia, 1947 in Slovakia, 1949 in Poland, and two years later in Croatia, to mention only a few countries in this region, was a part of the great worldwide upsurge of interest in Steinbeck following the novel's publication in the United States. Given that the novel uncompromisingly exposes and attacks the corruption and evils of capitalism, it is understandable that Steinbeck was received with enthusiasm as a politically progressive writer. His books were widely translated and used as a political tool against the social order of capitalism. Even more so was his criticism targeted at the United States, which—according to the prevailing socialist opinion of the time—symbolized all the vices of the corrupted West.

In Slovenia, for example, *The Grapes of Wrath* was crucial to the understanding of the working-class experience in America, and made Steinbeck a household name. Slovene people, living in a poor country in the process of building its own economy and politics, and asserting its national consciousness, could easily identify themselves with Steinbeck's rebels, who persist in their environment, struggle with it, and try to change it. However, to attribute the writer's appeal in Slovenia and in other countries of the Eastern bloc to the daring sincerity of his writing and to the passion he brought to his portraits of the common people is only half the story. The reasons for Steinbeck's specific position in the social and cultural history of these countries up to the present are complex, involving politics at least as much, if not more than his literary qualities. And to some degree the reasons transcend Steinbeck the person. Because of his anger and genuine sensitivity to human suffering, he ceased to be regarded as an individual and was assigned the status of a sympathetic advocate of the workers' cause. Steinbeck was particularly popular in the 1960s, with seventeen publications of his books in the former Czechoslovakian market alone, and fourteen in Poland.

The tendency to view Steinbeck mainly as a writer of protest novels, striving for equitable social conditions, may explain why his postwar works, showing a conspicuous change in fictional method and the author's exploration of new creative venues, have brought negative critical responses. The opinion that Steinbeck betrayed the working class by "ignoring the analysis of social conditions" and surrendered instead to "skeptical individualism" was expressed first by the influential Russian critic A. Starcev (133). The Slovene reviewer Marija Cvetko, among others, underrated *Travels with Charley.* "Many would be ashamed of this book," she claimed in 1964, and then went on to attack Steinbeck's "lukewarm personal involvement and the lack of intensity of his critical insight" (7). However, it was not until after the writer overtly showed his support for American involvement in Vietnam that his popularity faded in all East European countries. "He betrayed his principles and everything he had ever fought for," claimed Bulgarian writer Blaga Dimitrova, one of many opposing voices in the late 1960s (92). This keen sense of disappointment resulted in a lack of interest in Steinbeck's work. New Steinbeck editions were particularly scarce in the 1980s. While in Slovakia this was a Steinbeck-free decade, in the Czech Republic and in Poland only two books were published respectively. Interestingly, Slovenia excels with five Steinbeck editions then, but ranks last (together with Croatia) in the 1990s and in the current decade. Perhaps it was also because of the shared cultural trend in the 1980s among the writers and critics in Eastern Europe to refrain from politics and from expressing their ideological involvement or lack of it, and to reflect on and understand events with the help of philosophy, religion, and science instead, that Steinbeck, who was at that time still mainly known for his social criticism, failed to find his way onto the desks of the translators, publishers and literary historians.

Steinbeck's rehabilitation was slow, but consistent. At present, and although he is still poorly represented in literary history and criticism, there seems to be a level of acceptance for him: he is considerably widely translated and read again in most of the countries of the area under consideration, except in Croatia and Slovenia, where he is only slowly regaining his lost prestige. As for Slovenia, my recently published book, *Pripovednistvo Johna Steinbecka* (*The Narrative Prose of John Steinbeck*, 2006), and the numerous studies I have written since 2000 to draw readers' attention to the multi-layered structure and the universal relevance of Steinbeck's texts will hopefully fuel further critical debates and inspire new readings and new translations of his books. In the Czech Republic, on the other hand, the revival of interest in Steinbeck's works began soon after the end of the communist era (1948–1989). When I was doing research for this essay, I was startled to find that ten Czech editions of Steinbeck's books have appeared since the turn of the millennium. Poland, too, has developed a cultural environment conducive to the translations of Steinbeck works: nine of them (out of a total of sixty) have been published in the last six years. This number is even more impressive if compared to four translations in Slovakia and in Hungary respectively, two of them in Slovenia and the single example in Croatia. As for the Czech Republic, Petr Kopecký informs us that the state's control over the cultural scene had already begun to loosen in the 1960s. Since ideological readings of literature often gave way to the study of its aesthetic value, many Czech critics examined Steinbeck's topics in a more global and critical perspective and recognized the creative potential of his texts much earlier than critics in its neighboring communist countries. Consequently, Steinbeck's works already began to be extensively translated and read anew in the early 1990s, although the writer had been equally misinterpreted by communist critical readers and condemned by the country's cultural leaders for his support of the Vietnam War.

If we want to fully assess Steinbeck's popular appeal in the countries that during the Cold War were behind the Iron Curtain, a brief look at some other relevant statistics would not be amiss. While in the past, particularly in the immediate postwar years, publishers liked to choose Steinbeck's Depression-era novels because of the writer's social concern and critical attitude toward the American social and economic system, today they opt for works with different thematic and philosophical bearings. In most cases, these are the same texts which were once marginalized by the state-controlled critics who related the concept of literary greatness to the work's social and political implications. In Hungary, for example, the four recently published Steinbeck translations are *Burning Bright* (2002), *Cup of Gold* (2001), *East of Eden* (2001), and *The Pearl* (2000). For Slovakia these include *The Wayward Bus* (2002), two subsequent publications of *To a God*

Unknown (2003, 2004), and *Cannery Row* (2005). In Slovenia, two Steinbeck translations have recently been published: *East of Eden* (2005) and *Of Mice and Men* (2007). The most recent publications in Poland are *Once There Was a War* (2005) and *The Log from the Sea of Cortez* (2006); both were earlier unavailable to the non-English speaking population there.

Another shared characteristic in the reception of Steinbeck's works in Eastern Europe is poor publisher interest in his novel *The Moon Is Down* (1942). In contrast to Nazi-occupied Western Europe, where the book was met with an "extraordinarily positive reception," it did not receive much attention in Eastern Europe; in most countries it has not been reprinted since its first publication in the 1940s or 1950s (Coers xiii). Only in Poland was it followed by a second printing in 1995, while in Slovenia, on the other hand, it has not been translated to date.

Similarly, in this part of the world *In Dubious Battle* can be purchased only in second-hand book shops. In the Czech Republic, for example, the novel was translated in 1945 and in 1959; in Romania it has not been reprinted since its first publication in 1958; in Slovenia the only publication dates from 1952, while in Poland, Slovakia and Croatia, up to this point, it has not been translated. Since in the past decades literature was considered "one of the best paths to social progress, ultimately guiding social and political action," the book was obviously translated because of its international notoriety as communist propaganda, and was intended to be used as a perfect model for action (Guran 109). And it was, too, until the communists gleaned its full meaning. The Slovene critic Rapa Suklje, for example, enthusiastically writes that the novel "announces a bright future with justice, equality and humanity," and makes us believe that "such a future cannot be far ahead" (173–74). In the same article, Suklje sees the novel "as a social solution capable of subverting capitalism" (174). The communist rhetoric based on optimism and social realism is clearly seen also in a short accompanying text written by the Slovene translators, which reads that "the novel depicts the misery of homeless agricultural workers struggling for survival . . . after the capitalism thoroughly changed the once so an idyllic country" (Bordon, Furlan 245). No less suggestive have been the book's covers: in both the Slovene and the Czech editions they are remarkable for the clenched worker's fists, the symbol of the power of the labor force.

The reason for not giving the book further public attention also has to do with propaganda, although in a quite different sense. In Poland, for example, "they interpreted it as hostile and banned it"; in some other countries it was tactfully obliterated from the literary record (Lewis 30). In Slovenia, the only criticism leveled against Steinbeck's treatment of communism came from Stane Ivanc, who supported his unappreciative position by referring to "outraged French critics [who had] denounced Steinbeck for his false portrayal of communism" (7). Very much in the same vein, the Czech critic Miroslav Jindra did not fail to mention that Steinbeck "naturalistically and negatively distorts the characters of the communist organizers," while Vladimir Vendys and A. J. Sastný censured Steinbeck for not drawing "conclusions from the disturbing situation he had witnessed" and for knowing "only a distorted form of dialectical materialism" (Kopecký 85).

Much more can be said about how Steinbeck's progressive social thought inadvertently served the utopian communist model of social improvement in Eastern Europe. But even on such a narrow scale of comparison, and despite some differences which should more appropriately be regarded as a result of intellectual choice rather than of a shared intellectual project, it is not hard to see how similar socio-political circumstances in these countries accounted for similar responses to Steinbeck's works, both in the field of criticism and publishing activity. This brief account also suggests that Steinbeck's works do need and warrant new, thoughtful, text-oriented insight and reconsideration. Today the most notable East European critics (Matei Calinescu, Virgil Nemoianu, Mircea Martin, Mihai Spariosu, etc.) show a clear preference for aesthetic criteria in textual analysis, just as Harold Bloom, J. Hillis Miller and many other authorities in the field of literary criticism do, and are concerned with style and its potential to relate the text creatively to the world, rather than with the ideology embedded in the literary work. Thus, given Steinbeck's depth of insight into the human condition, his texts will inevitably make a convincing case for the importance of new readings of old texts.

WORKS CITED

Bloom, Harold. "Elegiac Conclusion." *Falling into Theory: Conflicting Views on Reading Literature.* Ed. David Richter. Boston/New York: Bedford/ St. Martin's, 2000. 225–35.

Bordon, Rado and Aljosa Furlan. "Beseda o Johnu Steinbecku." *Negotova bitka* (*In Dubious Battle*). By John Steinbeck. Trans. Aljosa Furlan and Rado Bordon. Ljubljana: Knjiznica Slovenskega Porocevalca, 1952. 245–46.

Cerce, Danica. *Pripovednistvo Johna Steinbecka*. Maribor: Mariborska literarna druzba, 2006.

Coers V., Donald. "Introduction." *The Moon Is Down*. By John Steinbeck. New York: Penguin Books, 1995. vii–xxiv.

Cvetko, Marija. "John Steinbeck: *Potovanje s Charleyjem*." *Tedenska tribuna* 24 Mar. 1964: 7.

Dimitrova, Blaga. "Odprto pismo gospodu Steinbecku." Trans. Katja Spurova. *Nasa zena* Mar. (1967): 91–93.

Guran, Letitia. "The Aesthetic Dimension of American-Romanian Comparative Literary Studies." *The Comparatist* 27 (May 2003): 94–116.

Ivanc, Stane. "Steinbeck—80 let prepozno." *Tedenska tribuna* 4 Dec. 1962: 7.

Kopecký, Petr. "The Story of John Steinbeck in Communist Czechoslovakia." *Steinbeck Studies* 16 (2005): 81–90.

Levine, George. "Reclaiming the Aesthetic." *Falling into Theory: Conflicting Views on Reading Literature*. Ed. David Richter. Boston/New York: Bedford/St. Martin's, 2000. 378–91.

Lewis, Cliff. "Art for Politics: John Steinbeck and FDR." *After 'The Grapes of Wrath': Essays on John Steinbeck*. Eds. Donald V. Coers, Paul D. Ruffin and Robert DeMott. Athens: Ohio UP, 1995. 23–39.

Mevlja, Dusan. "John Steinbeck: *Polentarska polica*." *Vecer* 23 Nov. 1953: 4.

Moder, Janko. "Spremna beseda o avtorju." *Grozdi jeze* (*The Grapes of Wrath*). By John Steinbeck. Trans. Janko Moder. Ljubljana: Cankarjeva zalozba, 1983. 587–610.

Nietzsche, Friedrich. *The Birth of Tragedy and Other Writings*. Ed. Raymond Geuss and Ronald Speirs. Trans. Ronald Speirs. Cambridge: Cambridge UP, 1999.

Nemoianu, Virgil. *A Theory of the Secondary: Literature, Progress, and Reaction*. Baltimore, London: John Hopkins UP, 1989

Starcev, A. "O socialnem realizmu v ZDA (About Social Realism in USA)." Trans. from Russian by Mile Klopcic. *Novi svet* 1–2 (1947) 130–37.

Suklje, Rapa. "John Steinbeck: *Negotova bitka*." *Nasa zena* 15 Aug. 1954: 173–74.

Turk, Joze. "Steinbeck in njegov raj." *Vzhodno od raja* (*East of Eden*). By John Steinbeck. Trans. Joze Turk. Ljubljana: Mladinska knjiga, 1980. 540–543.

10

John Steinbeck as Lyndon B. Johnson's Speech Writer

Tetsumaro Hayashi
Ball State University

In the 1960s John Steinbeck and Lyndon B. Johnson formed a unique moral and political alliance. As Jackson J. Benson states in his biography of Steinbeck, the seemingly spontaneous rapport between the two men blossomed from a casual acquaintanceship into an almost family-like relationship, with the Steinbecks being accorded red-carpet treatment at the White House during the Johnson administration. Friendship soon developed into an unshakable, loyal partisanship from 1964 to 1968—one of the most turbulent eras in American history.

John Steinbeck served not only as LBJ's occasional and quasi-official speech writer but also as political advisor, personal family friend, and pro-government journalist-spokesman. Nonetheless, unanswered questions revolve around their relationship. What speeches did he write for LBJ? Did Steinbeck's speeches ever influence Johnson's political ideologies and values? Did the President inspire Steinbeck to become a more politically active prose writer? This essay attempts to find answers to such crucial questions in order to discover not only the nature, extent, quality, and motivations of the moral and political alliance between Steinbeck and Johnson, but also to discern Steinbeck's concept of writing and speech communication—his views on the craftsmanship and artistry of writing during his involvement with the Johnson administration.

BACKGROUND OF THE RELATIONSHIP

In an April 16, 1964, letter to Jack Valenti, President Johnson's senior White House advisor, Steinbeck refers to a request to write a
biographical brochure of President Johnson for the 1964 presidential
campaign. The letter also states that Valenti's associate, Lloyd Wright,
phoned Steinbeck about the proposed statement, suggesting that he
limit it to 2,500 words, with a first draft to be compiled by May 1,
1964. In response to Wright's request, however, Steinbeck told Valenti
that he preferred a May 15 deadline. This reply demonstrates Steinbeck's serious commitment to the task, his thoroughness in exploring every possible means to portray President Johnson as humane,
empathetic, and trustworthy as he campaigned against Senator Barry
Goldwater, the Republican presidential candidate.

In order to achieve this goal, Steinbeck devised a variety of questions about Johnson in order to obtain every conceivable source of
information about the President for the biography. Steinbeck sent the
list of questions to Valenti, who must subsequently have provided
various answers, responses, and suggestions, along with photographs
of the President and a list of childhood friends in Texas. The author's
handwritten notes, entitled, "Notes and Questions for JV about LBJ,"
reveal Steinbeck's all-out effort to prepare the biography and his
serious attempt to know LBJ as thoroughly and dimensionally as
possible —as a human being, a family man, a political leader, and
President of the United States. These questions also suggest Steinbeck's
basic three-part design for the brochure—Part I: the chronological
narrative about LBJ; Part II: the image of LBJ as a likeable, decent human being; and Part III: the conclusion based on Parts I and II. In the
memo to Valenti, Steinbeck asked numerous questions—forty-two to
be specific—to prepare the biography; these questions were followed
by more commentaries and questions about the President. Judging
from the letter, Steinbeck must have kept Valenti and his research as-
sistants extremely busy providing him with precise answers, pertinent
sources of information, and appropriate anecdotes for the relatively
brief campaign biography.

The voluminous list of questions—ranging from queries concerning
LBJ's musical and reading tastes, to his concern for people and the environment, to his attitude towards fishing and hunting, and more—seem
to illustrate Baruch Spinoza's statement: "What Paul says about Peter

was more about Paul than about Peter" (56). This observation is especially appropriate when one considers other questions on Steinbeck's list that arise not from political concern but from sheer self-interest. For example, in other questions he asks, "What is his feeling about money? . . . Does he . . . pick flowers? . . . Is he generous?" Yes, they testify to Steinbeck's creative mind and writing process during the time he worked on the LBJ biography. As he once told Valenti in a June 15, 1965, letter, "Writing is my trade, my profession, and my obsession."

In a letter to Valenti, dated May 4, 1964, Steinbeck wrote, "The enclosed are working copies, entitled 'A President—Not a Candidate.' If you and the Central Committee do not want this piece or can't use it, do not hesitate to throw it out. . . . If changes are to be made, I'm giving as much time as possible. . . . I'll be glad to change or to cut anything." Although a reputable writer at the time, Steinbeck was humbly cooperative, willing to comply with requests from Valenti, Johnson, and their writing task force.

Jack Valenti responded to this letter on May 11, 1964, with the assurance that it had met the President's wholehearted approval:

> I can only tell you that the President personally read your draft. But yesterday he told me that your piece was the finest work of writing that he has ever read that dealt with the personal man of Lyndon B. Johnson. . . . At any rate, it is a marvelous piece of draftsmanship which only confirms the catalogue of American opinion about John Steinbeck. You will be hearing more from me shortly, but I did want you to know what the President had to say about your draft.

On May 12, 1964, Steinbeck wrote again to Valenti, sending him also a sixteen-page, double-spaced revised manuscript of "A President—Not a Candidate." Steinbeck prefaced the draft with a memo: "As it happens this gets in just under the deadline. I'll rush [it] out to you."

The revised draft of the biography has three parts, according to a previously suggested format: a narrative account of LBJ's life, the image of the President, and a conclusion.

The narrative section begins with a definition of the American heritage, deriving from the insight and foresight of our forefathers, which had been "proof not only against foreign attack, but against our own stupidities which are sometimes more dangerous"—a statement later revised and included in Steinbeck's *America and Americans* (1966). It continues with a discussion of the significance and impact

of changes in American society and its future and the people's attitude toward these changes, maintaining that "the United States must
change to meet change, accommodate when possible and resist when
compromise plays out," and "Americans must accept and encourage
change within, social and economic and spiritual, and these things
must be done within the equation of our country which has served
us so well."

Curiously, this theme of change echoes throughout Presidential
campaigns and political propaganda since Steinbeck and LBJ—with
resounding, reverberating rhetoric, sometimes with little substance.
Anxious to please, Steinbeck has followed the prescribed formula, at
least in this instance. As Steinbeck biographer Jackson J. Benson notes,
Steinbeck "probably became too involved with the Johnson White
House and lost some independence of mind as it conflicted with stronger impulses of duty to country and loyalty to friends" (958).

Defining the concept of the American Presidency, Steinbeck
is more specific both in the May 1964 letter to Valenti and in
"A President—Not a Candidate": "We require a President who knows
not only his own job, but also all the other branches of government.
. . . We require a President who knows every facet and foible of America and the world outside our boundaries." Steinbeck then delineates
in some detail how ideally Lyndon B. Johnson had already fulfilled
and also how he would continue to fulfill such demanding qualifica-
tions and complex requirements—how competently he had already
proved himself to be an exemplary President of the United States.

Having described the unique, paradoxical relationship between
the U.S. President and the U.S. citizens, Steinbeck vividly portrayed
the caliber of LBJ, using the question-answer method with which he
had begun his research and beginning with his passions and likes.
His passions include an ardent belief in the American government,
his own work in it, and a tireless involvement in life. But his likes
center primarily around life on his ranch, with its "ties to his youth,
his childhood, and to his ancestry." There he enjoys "improving and
managing it"; riding his horse; hunting, but not "for sport"; restoring
"his vitality by staying . . . for a few days."

The question "How Does He Work?" centers around a similarly
deep passion for government, with LBJ's expecting his cohorts to share
his own deep concern. A workaholic himself, he is "a slave driver." He
"demands perfection, and his helpers do their best to give it to him."

He "excuses a first mistake, considering it a lesson, but he is merciless to the man who fails to learn and makes the same mistake twice." LBJ has "a passion for learning" and "listens carefully to all ideas and opinions and in many cases, uses them after careful consideration." To the loyal worker, he "gives unlimited loyalty and affection."

The question "Is He Generous?" reflects the President's passionate nature as well: He is "impulsively generous." He "loves to give presents and they go to high officers and to the girls of his secretarial staff."

"What Does He Hate?" elicited an altruistic response: He "hates gossip and cruelty." "Abuse or brutality to women and children drive him to rage."

"Is He Sensitive to Criticism of Himself?" again reveals generosity of spirit: "Not if it is deserved—not if he can learn from it." "Untruth, critical innuendo, secret and malicious attacks that have the quality of gossip"—these "puzzle him and trouble him," because "he is incapable of them in himself."

"What Does He Read?" reveals his strong social interests: "history, sociology, economics, and some biography."

The question "What Is His Favorite Pastime?" also shows the President to be socially motivated: It is definitely "discussion" as "a part of his passion for learning." He learns "through discussion with men and women in many fields." He "asks questions and listens to answers and remembers." He "absorbs facts, ideas, possibilities, and people." His spectacular success as a Senate leader "was the result not only of study and experience in the rules and techniques of the Senate, but also of his intimate knowledge and evaluation of the individual senators." LBJ knew well that government is certainly made by law, but it is interpreted and administered by human beings. Very early on, he "learned that it is necessary to understand both." His favorite quotation from Isaiah 1:18 reflects this desire to communicate: "Come now and let us reason together."

To the question "What Is His Greatest Talent As a Statesman?" Steinbeck responds that it is "the ability to use his knowledge of men and events in conjunction with his highly developed sense of timing."

Ardently believing in LBJ's capacity to lead, Steinbeck responds to the question "Will He Be Known As a Great President?" most positively: "If he continues to perform as he has in his first half year, he will be known as one of the greatest."

In his conclusion to "A President—Not a Candidate," Steinbeck discussed Presidential power, which he regarded as

> a moral power activated by persuasion, by discussion, by the manipulation and alignment of many small, but aggressive forces—each weak in itself, but protected by the law from usurpation of its rights and punitive action against it by the Executive.

And he reiterated one of the imperatives for a President: "The President must have exact and sensitive knowledge not only of his own office, but of all the other branches of government, if his program is to progress at all." Steinbeck observed how competently LBJ had

> established a stable and efficient administration and impressed the nation with his leadership after John F. Kennedy's assassination. His actions and accomplishments during his 175 days have been astonishing and unprecedented, . . . the result of great and increasing skill.

Steinbeck ended his draft with the declaration that

> history is moving too fast for America to indulge in the circus of candidacy, baby-patting, blintz-eating, handpumping, the tricks. . . . America wants not a candidate but a President. And we have a President.

STEINBECK'S DRAFT OF LBJ'S ACCEPTANCE SPEECH

In addition to writing this campaign biography—in itself a momentous task—LBJ asked Steinbeck to write at least three speeches for him. Steinbeck's letter to Jack Valenti on June 6, 1964, states, "As you well know, the President asked me to do certain things concerning the coming campaign. Of course, I shall be very glad to do this. But I have a few very simple requests." Once again, Steinbeck took LBJ's requests seriously and devoted ardent attention to them. One of the three speeches to which he referred was to be given in San Francisco, one in Los Angeles, and the final one at the convention as his acceptance speech. Steinbeck asked Valenti to provide taped speech drafts in order to save time, to give him a sense of the specific audiences and occasions for the speeches, and to name the vice presidential candidate so the acceptance speech (the one he regarded as most important) could be geared to him as well. In the same letter Steinbeck stated that he would fulfill all of these assignments, with a curious note about finances: "Since it is not possible for me to contribute financially to the campaign, I can only offer time and what talent I may have. But I should like it understood that I pay my own expenses."

Jackson J. Benson details the background of events at the White House at the time Steinbeck was preparing LBJ's acceptance speech:

> When the Steinbecks were with the Johnsons, they were treated almost like members of the family. They stayed near the Johnsons on the second floor in the Queen's Bedroom or the Lincoln Room, and were able to have breakfast in the little office where Lincoln often breakfasted. When Steinbeck was asked to work on Johnson's acceptance speech, the materials came to him on Long Island by military airplane, and when they went to the White House to be with the Johnsons during the first few days of the convention, so that John could further polish the speech, a plane came to pick them up. (957)

Steinbeck's devotion to the President and to the assigned writing tasks show him to be deserving of such favored treatment by the White House. In a June 12, 1964, letter to Valenti, Steinbeck expressed the difficulties and frustrations he was experiencing in preparation for LBJ's acceptance speech, shared the agony of having to write it under pressure, and attached the "second draft" of the speech, asking Valenti to edit it.

Steinbeck's four-page draft of LBJ's acceptance speech consists of twenty-seven short paragraphs for clarity, easy reading, and editorial review. When one compares this draft with the finally printed "Acceptance Speech," there appears at first glance to be a dramatic contrast. After careful review and analysis of the two texts, however, one is struck by Steinbeck's considerable influence on the writing task force and even more importantly on LBJ's political philosophy, which Steinbeck articulately spelled out in the printed text. Specifically and accurately he identified LBJ's basic political philosophy in colorful, candid metaphors and episodes. In this draft he emphasized the following major points:

1. The political commitment is mutual—involving both the nominee and those who nominated him. The Presidential candidate and the Democratic delegates who nominated him for the Presidency must offer their utmost dedication to the country.
2. Echoing John F. Kennedy's famous chiastic line "Ask not what your country can do for you—ask what you can do for your

country," in Johnson's speech Steinbeck offers an interpretation: "You put in more than you take out" to enrich our country—a premise later expanded and discussed in *America and Americans*, encouraging Americans to look toward a responsible and ethical future and to embark on a path with "direction," "purpose," and "a joy of anticipation" (142).

3. Steinbeck's draft reminds us of the ultimate value structure: "The nation takes precedence over the party; the people are more important than the person; and the country is greater than its parts," and "America is more precious and more dear than any section of it"—a translation of his own group-man concept into political philosophy, a topic to be taken up again in *America and Americans* (9).

4. Steinbeck's draft asserts that the American people should not fear change but should grow with it because they live in a dynamic society in a dynamic age, as "I (the President) will welcome it, test it, and if it works, use it." The draft maintains further that this is "the traditional American way of doing things," again an essential idea to be further developed in *America and Americans*:

> In one or two, certainly not more than three generations each ethnic group has clicked into place in the union without losing the *pluribus*. When we read the line-up of a University of Notre Dame football team, called the "Fighting Irish," we do not find it ridiculous that the names are Polish, Slovak, Italian, or Fiji, for that matter. They *are* the Fighting Irish. (14)

5. The greatness of the White House derives from "the minds and souls and influence of great men."

6. The future holds both "dangerous challenges" and "possibilities," and we must explore the full potentials and possibilities among us and around us in the sea, on the land, and in the sky.

7. We must learn to protect ourselves from dangers, to use leisure creatively and positively, to overcome racial prejudices, and to fight against ignorance, disease, poverty, and drugs—again Steinbeck's significant motifs in *America and Americans*.

8. We must learn to balance our budget to remain economically sound and strong, while preserving our international leadership among nations.

9. Steinbeck concludes the draft of LBJ's acceptance speech by declaring that the nomination means "a social contract" between the nominee and those who put him there—democratic "partici-

pation, preoccupation, and effort toward a government which intends to open a . . . door on a bright and shining future."

As LBJ's civilian advisor as well as his speech writer, Steinbeck continued to express his concern about the effectiveness of LBJ's Presidential speeches, and top White House aides regarded Steinbeck as one of the finest communication experts—one like Whitman's "Inner Communicant." Apparently Steinbeck liked this identity, generously sharing his expertise as an artist and craftsman in communications with LBJ's top advisors.

Among delicate political matters, in an audiotape to Valenti, dated June 15, 1964, Steinbeck discussed audience-speaker rapport and the intricate art of speech communication—placing himself in the position of one who gives advice to rulers. In this audiotape Steinbeck suggested that LBJ address one specific person in the audience, thus making the speech effectively and personally appealing to that individual—reminiscent of his advice on making writing effective by addressing it to one particular person.

As for the speech writing, Steinbeck advised, it should be delivered "in short, simple, sentences," each one of which should be understood on first hearing, for "if it doesn't make an impact, the audience has been lost." LBJ's speech should be delivered with "the rhythms which communicate," using his "own rhythm and vernacular" rather than that of the speech writer. Steinbeck insisted that "the speech and the man should be identical." The speech itself, he concluded, should always be "short, simple, exact, and memorable."

In this same audiotape, Steinbeck also offered advice for the upcoming acceptance speech, suggesting what should be included as Johnson accepts the trust and confidence of his people, for he is also accepting

> loneliness and the black hours of decision, of accusation for fancied faults, of opposition by irresponsible opponents, of denunciation by screwballs, and actually, he is accepting exhaustion and putting his life in danger when he goes out in public.

He further takes on "work beyond a man's ability," together with "heartbreak and sadness." He is taking on himself "the death of soldiers—the hunger of children, the failures of the economy—bankruptcy of business, all of those he takes on himself." Steinbeck's advocacy for the President is here revealed in sympathy, compassion, and admiration.

In this audiotape Steinbeck goes further, asking and answering the question of what the President expects of himself: that he will "do the best that he can do in any given situation and in any moment," expecting of himself "the ability to keep alive the greatness of our past, the integrity of our government, the justice of the court, and the ethics of the executive." He must work, too, to "navigate the ugly and dangerous waters of international tensions and to enlarge the entirely new concept that one nation cannot succeed alone," while diligently remaining "aware of the dangers from without."

In return, Steinbeck maintains, the President must establish expectations for his countrymen—ranging from responsibility to creativity in science and government. Calling these ideas and suggestions "an outline" with "various subjects and headings," into which the acceptance speech could go, Steinbeck asked Valenti whether he needed information on "any other fields, directions, ideas, or subjects that needed to be included" before he undertook the final writing of the acceptance speech. These suggestions, to some extent, may be connected to Johnson's own idea of the Great Society, with its five principles (Johnson 172–73):

1. to employ our power purposefully, although always with great restraint
2. to control, to reduce, and ultimately to eliminate the modern engines of destruction
3. to support these associations of nations which reflect the opportunities and necessities of the modern world
4. to encourage the right of each people to govern themselves and shape their own institution
5. to help improve the life of man

DRAFT OF LBJ'S INAUGURAL SPEECH

In his undated audiotape to Jack Valenti, which must have been sent about July or August of 1964, Steinbeck proposed essential ideas to be included in the inaugural speech. As for the nature of an inaugural, which will become "the trademark, the shield, and the direction" of the country, it should attempt "to light some kind of fire." It should also be "a highly emotional speech—one that people feel rather than listen to," and the oath should be "short, awesome, and awe-inspiring."

The Constitution should be the President's guide, Steinbeck wrote, because it is "the will of the people" and "the mandate of the people," and because it declares "what we are, what we hope to be, and what we intend to be." Outlining in brief the nature of the Constitution and of the President's responsibility to uphold it, Steinbeck then defines the United States as "the product of powerful . . . and hopeful people. . . . We have the power, the imagination, and the technique for exploring our own world first and other worlds second." He declares furthermore that we must "explore our minds and our impulses to the end that we may be truly equal in opportunity."

The President's responsibility toward attaining these goals was to use every avenue toward "peace, understanding, and brotherhood among nations" during a challenging and dangerous time. Steinbeck addressed as well the basic ideas of the Great Society; Civil Rights; the country's moral responsibility as the guardian of atomic power; and the war against poverty, ignorance, and prejudice. He concluded his audiotape to Valenti and his thoughts for the inaugural message with a proclamation: "On these terms of joyous emancipation, let the waves of the future be a tidal wave of hope, creativeness, and optimism." Again in an audiotape, on August 14, 1964, Valenti responded to Steinbeck's letter:

> The material you sent was just right. You did a marvelous job of giving it body and form and some soul. I have stripped all identification and have now passed it along to the others on our platform writing task force. I would hope to put in the mail today an outline of an acceptance speech. It was wonderful seeing you and Elaine and thank you so much, my good friend, for your prompt response to our call for assistance.

This audiotape typifies the extraordinarily congenial working relationship between Steinbeck and Jack Valenti—bound together by their mutual loyalty and friendship with LBJ. It reveals as well Steinbeck's substantial ideological influence on LBJ's political philosophy, including his favorite Great Society initiative. And it reveals, too, something about Steinbeck as a writer. In particular, it demonstrates his thoroughness and his absorption in all aspects of the writing task—from audience appeal, to the ethos of the speaker, to the specific diction for the rhetorical task.

In comparing Steinbeck's proposed ideas for the inaugural address in the draft with the printed text of LBJ's "Inaugural Address," a reader discovers the President's extensive adoption (both in ideology and enunciation) of Steinbeck's own political, social, economic, ecological, spiritual, and moral values—evocatively reflecting the democratic principles of the country's forebears in moving metaphors and colorful episode (many of these to be richly expanded and elaborated in *America and Americans*). According to Valenti, the "Inaugural Address" adopted verbatim one of Steinbeck's dynamic definitions of the Great Society: "I do not believe that the Great Society is the ordered, changeless, and sterile battalion of the ants. It is the excitement of becoming—always becoming, trying, probing, falling, resting, and trying again—but always trying and always gaining." Steinbeck's definition was later expanded and modified in LBJ's *This America* (1966).

CONCLUSION

As I reviewed letters exchanged between John Steinbeck and Jack Valenti and other primary documents concerning the author's dedication to the task of serving as LBJ's speech writer, several facts became clear. Following his service as political advisor (and friend) to Adlai E. Stevenson in the 1950s, John Steinbeck became John F. Kennedy's cultural ambassador to Russia in 1962–63. After JFK's assassination, Steinbeck offered his advice and assistance to the new President. Johnson and his wife, Lady Bird, accepted Steinbeck's offer appreciatively and seriously, recognizing Steinbeck's fame, popularity, and talent as a Nobel Prize laureate and also as a close friend of Adlai Stevenson—a man trusted by loyalists in the Democratic Party. The Johnsons liked as well Steinbeck's willingness to defend the President with patriotic fervor.

As LBJ's advisor, Steinbeck, had been asked to use his gift as a writer to help the President communicate effectively with the general public—prospective voters—especially during the Presidential campaign against Senator Barry Goldwater in the early 1960s. On occasion at the President's direct request but more often through Jack Valenti (who was in charge of communications), Steinbeck offered his time, talent, and creative (if sometimes unorthodox) ideas and suggestions in the hope of insuring political victory in Johnson's campaign for President.

A writer sensitively conscious of the craft of writing and effective communication, Steinbeck advised LBJ technically and rhetorically on how to improve the delivery of presidential speeches and how to gain greater rapport with the voters and general public. Steinbeck was eventually won over by LBJ and acceded to requests to write more speeches than initially expected, always dedicating himself to each writing task by thorough and extensive research through critical revisions to perfect the draft for LBJ.

An artist in writing and communication and a "minstrel" in prose writing, Steinbeck knew well the vital importance of "sound, sight, and sense." He always strove to observe the decorum of just the right fit between the speaker and the speech and to find that diction and style that produced a fine, musical, flowing prose most likely to win over an audience. As speech writer and advocate, he created a pleasing "smoothness, coordination, and rhythm all together." The energy spent as public servant to the President were not wasted. For later Steinbeck developed many of his political ideologies and opinions into refined essays in *America and Americans* (1966)—his own moral, political vision of America.

It seems safe to say at this point, therefore, that LBJ as President inspired Steinbeck's political awareness, thinking, and writing while Steinbeck enforced, focused, and articulated LBJ's idealistic, political philosophy and helped him develop the means by which to preach the gospel of the Great Society more effectively to the American people. In a sense, Steinbeck might be viewed as a spokesman for American political values as he performed his moral and social duty as a Nobel Prize laureate, as a patriotic American journalist, and as a novelist of worldwide prominence. Because he had already been a politically active writer when he supported Adlai Stevenson in the 1950s, Steinbeck's passionate support of LBJ was also a spontaneous outcome of his political engagement in the destiny of his beloved country in the 1950s and 1960s.[1]

NOTE

1. I did extensive, intensive, funded research on John Steinbeck and Lyndon Johnson at the Lyndon B. Johnson Presidential Library, Austin, Texas, and at the University of Texas Graduate Library, Austin, Texas, during

five summer research visits there. All unpublished materials cited are from these libraries.

WORKS CITED

Benson, Jackson J. *The True Adventures of John Steinbeck, Writer.* New York: Viking Press, 1974.

Johnson, Lyndon B. *This America.* New York: Random House, 1966.

Spinoza, Baruch. In Erich Fromm's *Psychoanalysis and Religion.* New Haven: Yale University Press, 1950.

Steinbeck, Elaine and Robert Wallsten, eds. New York: Viking Press, 1975.

Steinbeck, John. "Acceptance Speech," a four-page draft, typed in single space.

——. *America and Americans.* New York: Viking Press, 1966.

——. JS/JV letter, April 16, 1964.

——. S/JV, a handwritten memo, "Notes and Questions," n.d.

——. S/JV, June 15, 1965.

——. S/JV, May 4, 1964.

——. S/JV, May 12. 1964.

——. JS/JV, June 6, 1964.

——. JS/JV, June 12, 1964.

——. JS/JV, audiotape, n.d.

——. JV/JS, August 14, 1964.

——. JS/Pascal Covici, Jr., April 13, 1956, 528.

——. "A President—Not a Candidate," a sixteen-page draft, double spaced.

Part 5

STEINBECK, CULTURE, VIEWPOINTS, A GRAND JOKE, AND A MEDITATIVE READING

Steinbeck's works, when placed within the concept of frontier and culture, provide a new perspective on the definitions of those terms. More importantly, this cultural frontier of wholeness and connections to both nature and other human beings is still open, not only for Americans but also for humanity.

—Luchen Li

11

John Steinbeck's Cultural Frontiers

Luchen Li
Kettering University

According to Terry Eagleton, "culture" is one of the two or three most complex words in the English language, a term which is sometimes considered to be the opposite of "nature." Etymologically speaking, "culture" is a concept derived from nature. Nature produces culture which changes nature. Culture is a matter of the human being's self-realization. The terms we often use—cultural wars, multiculturalism, cross-cultural communications—represent tribal and societal differences. In Latin, "colere" means anything from cultivating and inhabiting to worshipping and protecting. For the sake of the argument in this article, I would like to highlight two aspects of culture. One is the human being's self-realization in front of Nature, and the other is the essential existence, or survival circumstance, of groups of people of various ethnicities. These two aspects of culture are elaborated in a number of Steinbeck's works.

Because the goal of this article is to discover Steinbeck's "cultural frontier," now let us define the term "frontier" and add it to our context. When we think of the term "frontier," images of axes, horses, guns, wagons or pioneers fighting with the native inhabitants come to our mind. The American frontier always reminds us of an area of free land, its continuous recession, and the advance of the American settlement westward. Hence, historian Frederick Jackson Turner announced in 1893 that the American frontier had been closed because no more land was left to be conquered and acquired.

However, Turner's view of the West is not what Steinbeck had in mind when depicting characters in his stories, most of which take place in the American West, but from a different point of view. He portrays a type of frontier which was still open in his times, and which I think is still open today. I would call it the "cultural frontier." Indeed, Steinbeck has exposed many cultural values which often contradict conventional beliefs—for example, those on society, government, religion, and human beings' relationship to nature. Steinbeck has intentionally created characters who fight against nature and struggle with themselves. Turner's concept of the frontier was mono-perspective, excluding the many social changes that happened after the Westward surge. Turner's error lies in his ethnocentric and nationalistic definition of the term "frontier," which in his mind, is the meeting point between savagery and civilization" and "the line of most effective and rapid Americanization." His claim of the closure of the frontier was based on his notion that the struggle with wilderness turned Europeans into Americans, a process which Turner made the central story of American history.

To some extent, Turner's view of the American West and the frontier marry well with James Fenimore Cooper's depictions of the fighting between the pioneers and the American Indians. When Turner claimed that the western frontier had closed, his frontier meant the geographical line on which the Europeans from the east coast had reached the very west of the continent. This account of history usually leaves out other key characters; accounts of women, the Spanish and Chinese settlers, and Native Americans were rarely heard of in early American literature. By contrast, Steinbeck's fiction, rather than describing how the easterners conquer the West, shows how the pioneers encounter and interact with the native people in the West and how the pioneers' own values and beliefs are shaped by their experience with the people who are already there. Joseph Wayne and his family in *To a God Unknown* and Adam Trask in *East of Eden*, among others, are such examples of assimilation. Steinbeck has illustrated striking sets of examples and counterexamples to illustrate, through realistic and sometimes biographical stories, a different perspective of the West that reveals that region's cultural and philosophical riches. To best perceive the cultural frontier in Steinbeck's works, we may look into the relationship between human beings and the land and with one another through some of the characters in his novels.

Steinbeck's fiction constitutes the most ambitious and thorough examination of the American ideal of humanizing the land and civilizing the country, with California as a major symbol of a promised land. On this vast landscape, Steinbeck draws a panorama of people living on and struggling for this modern land of promise, which is, in truth, a wasteland. In so doing, he exposes a conflict between human beings and nature.

In the belief of many early pioneers, God left the American West arid in order to challenge and reform America. Thus, transforming the West, its land, forest, and desert into a garden became a holy task. A typical colonial picture of the westering movement is of the pioneers as conquerors, whereas the Great West, as non-life and therefore the "other," was wild and empty. The West was therefore a natural "object" for human beings to take, to exploit, and even to abuse. The pioneers welcomed wild country as a challenge. Men conceived of themselves as agents of God in the regenerating process that turned the perceived ungodly and useless into a beneficent civilization. Such an attitude prompted both pioneers and writers to use military metaphors to discuss the coming of civilization. Writers and historians of westward expansion wrote about wilderness as an "enemy" which had to be "conquered," "subdued," and "anguished" by a "pioneer army." As such, humans and wilderness were locked in mortal combat.[1]

To many, like Frederick J. Turner, the West is the outer edge of society and wilderness, a frontier, "the meeting point of savagery and civilization." In his famous essay "The Significance of the Frontier in American History" (1893), Turner makes it clear that the wildness of the country is its most basic ingredient and the essential formative influence on the national character. Although he believes that the pioneer transforms the wilderness, he has to agree that "the wilderness masters the colonist" as well. Turner's concept has influenced many writers and formed the traditional mindset of most Americans. In the works of Robert Frost, Robinson Jeffers, Jack London, and Wallace Stevens, to illustrate, wilderness often appears dark, inhuman, malevolent, and desirable.

Steinbeck sees this conflict between humans and nature and exposes the westering impulse as a material desire for more. As Joseph Wayne in *To a God Unknown* and Adam Trask in *East of Eden* seem to show us, the desire of conquering the land indicates our human instinct to tame and civilize the "other," the wilderness. Eden in both these novels is merely a small farm characterized by abundance, purity and simplicity until its agrarian tenants, such as Joseph Wayne and Adam Trask, recognize some awkwardly polarized contradictions (such as good and evil) that are set against the backdrop of the pastoral hope to reclaim the lost simplicity of a classical Golden Age, a biblical garden, a rural landscape.

However, while many writers portray the West as a place for people to act on their dominant relationship with nature, Steinbeck invokes an opposite rhetoric. In *To a God Unknown* Joseph Wayne serves as a Christian pioneer to fight the wilderness in order to make his new homestead. At the beginning of the story, Steinbeck describes him as a pioneer anxious to march to the West. Answering his father's call, Joseph says, "The land [in the West] is being taken. . . . If I wait, the good land might all be taken. I've a hunger for the land, sir." And "his eyes had grown feverish with the hunger," writes Steinbeck (176–177). When recounting the history of Central California at the beginning of *The Pastures of Heaven*, Steinbeck presents a similar picture of humans hungry for land, describing the figure of a man who is to start the history of this region: "He whose rapacious manhood was building a new race for California, this bearded, savage bearer of civilization slipped from his saddle and took off his steel hat. 'Holy Mother!' he whispered. 'Here are the green pastures of Heaven to which our Lord leadeth us'" (3–4). Noticeable is the irony with which Steinbeck describes this pioneer as a "savage bearer of civilization." But the "bearer of civilization" and "civilization," in Steinbeck's view, are totally different things. The pioneer, a human figure, does not stand for civilization; rather he is still as savage as pagans. Yet this savage being, superior as he thinks he is to all others—animals, the land, rivers and mountains in the wilderness—always has a reason to possess and control the "others." Many pioneers move to the West because, as they claim, the "Lord" and "God" want them to conquer the wild and to Christianize savagery. Regarding wilderness as a dark and sinister symbol, they share the long Western tradition of imagining wild country as a moral vacuum, a cursed and chaotic wasteland (Nash 24). So frontiersmen battled wild country not only for personal survival but in the name of nation, race, and God. As Roderick Nash has explained, civilizing the West meant enlightening darkness, ordering chaos, and changing evil into good. In the morality play of westward expansion, wilderness was the villain, and the pioneer was the hero (25). Steinbeck thus writes of Joseph:

> As he looked into the valley, Joseph felt his body flushing with a hot fluid of love. "This is mine," he said simply, and his eyes sparkled with tears and his brain was filled with wonder that this should be his. . . . He felt that the trees were his children and the land his child. For a moment he seemed to float high in the air and to look down upon it. "It's mine," he said again, "and I must take care of it." (181)

At this moment, Joseph is no longer thinking of the land as soil; he regards it as a sensuous woman. His possessiveness becomes a passion:

> He stamped his feet into the soft earth. Then the exultance grew to be a sharp pain of desire that ran through his body in a hot river. He flung himself face downward on the grass and pressed his cheek against the wet stems. His fingers gripped the wet grass and tore it out, and gripped again. His thighs beat heavily on the earth. . . . For a moment the land had been his wife. (182–183)

Regardless of his desires, Joseph Wayne eventually fails to achieve his dreams of conquering the land, or nature, so to speak. The finale of the novel reminds us rather that he is claimed by nature.

In Steinbeck's view, the civilized world's discontent with its status quo and desire for more material possessions have turned human beings into devourers, monsters raking the lives of lesser creatures into an insatiable maw (Timmerman 198). Avarice and destructiveness, to Steinbeck, are precisely the nature of human civilization, a point he makes clear when he describes the town in animalistic imagery: "A town is a thing like a colonial animal. A town has a nervous system and a head and shoulders and feet. A town is a thing separate from all other towns, so that there are no two towns alike. And a town has a whole emotion" (32). In his later novels, Steinbeck continues to examine the emotion and sensuousness of human beings who live in their towns or on their land or farm. *Cannery Row, Of Mice and Men, Tortilla Flat,* and *East of Eden,* for example, are among such works.

The people in *Cannery Row* seem to forget their sorrows and troubles and enjoy life as it *is,* living in harmony with nature. As Steinbeck writes of his characters,

> Mack and the boys, too, [are] spinning in their orbits. They are the Virtues, the Graces, the Beauties of the hurried mangled craziness of

Monterey and the cosmic Monterey where men in fear and hunger
destroy their stomachs in the fight to secure certain food, where men
hungering for love destroy everything lovable about them. (14–15)

Indeed, reading Steinbeck's works, we view the following pictures.
Monterey was still a land of Indians and Mexicans and Spaniards, a
land of great forests, mountainous ridges hiding mines of gold and
silver, and fertile valleys that eventually yielded the richest lode of
all—vegetables. Cannery Row is a lazy bustle, punctuated by the
frantic clanging of cannery bells, the shrill noise of their steam valves,
and the lazy movements of fishermen casting lines along the shore
in the evening. In came the Italians, Mexicans, Portuguese, Japanese,
and Chinese, each in separate living areas. And the ethnically diverse
population of Monterey converged in many ways. In *Cannery Row*,
Steinbeck creates a world which is characterized by its rich variety, its
benevolent disorder:

Cannery Row is a poem, a stink, a grating noise, a quality of light, a
tone, a habit, a nostalgia, a dream . . . tin and iron and rust and splin-
tered wood, chipped pavement and weedy lots and junk heaps, sardine
canneries. (5)

This is exactly what Steinbeck envisions as the beauty of life in the
West where the orthodox order from the east coast is disrupted and
displaced. Steinbeck provides us with a pastoral Cannery Row in his
fictional account, describing in the "bums" one of the most basic
attributes imputed to simple men: "Mack and the boys know everything that has ever happened in the world and possibly everything
that will happen" (130). In the same conversation involving Doc,
Steinbeck, like the British Romantic Wordsworth, links this attribute
with the primitive:

The things we admire in men, kindness and generosity, openness,
honesty, understanding and feeling are the concomitants of failure in
our system. And those traits we detest, sharpness, greed, acquisitiveness, meanness, egotism and self-interest are the traits of success. And
while men admire the quality of the first they love the produce of the
second.
    "Who wants to be good if he has to be hungry too?" said Richard
Frost.
    "Oh, it isn't a matter of hunger. It's something quite different. The
sale of souls to gain the whole world is completely voluntary and almost

unanimous—but not quite. Everywhere in the world there are Mack and the boys. I've seen them in an ice cream seller in Mexico and in an Aleut in Alaska." (131)

Steinbeck thus shows that Mac and the boys incorporate the whole world by holding it more or less passively as a complex but unified object of contemplation. In the preface to *Tortilla Flat*, the author explains the story's Arthurian roots:

> For Danny's house was not unlike the Round Table [of King Arthur], and Danny's friends were not unlike the knights of it. And this is the story of how that group came into being, of how it flourished and grew to be an organization beautiful and wise. This story deals with the adventures of Danny's friends, with the good they did, with their thoughts and their endeavors. In the end, this story tells how the talisman was lost and how the group disintegrated.

As shown with the code of life in his fiction, Steinbeck looks for alternatives, which might encourage the better survival of human beings within society and a larger system. Different from the tragic characters in works such as *To a God Unknown* and *East of Eden*, Steinbeck portrays the comedies of life in *Cannery Row* and *Tortilla Flat*. The characters in the latter are adorable even though they may be "weak," stupid, and undignified as perceived by traditional western minds. As tragic heroes suffer or die for their ideas and desires, comic heroes survive without them.

Another aspect of the cultural frontier in Steinbeck's works lies in the perplexing interaction and conflict among social and ethnic groups. During the years Steinbeck was planning *East of Eden*, he was curiously preoccupied with the Taoist concept of the inseparability of such oppositions as good and evil, strength and weakness, love and hate, and beauty and ugliness. He strongly believed that neither side of such doubles can exist without the other.

In *East of Eden* Steinbeck uses the Cain-Abel story but tells it in a framework of Eastern philosophy. The novel presents a theme based on Steinbeck's reinterpretation of the Bible story; yet, the value derived from this reinterpretation is often unclear if it is simply read as a Bible review. As Peter Lisca points out with regret, despite the excessive and obvious parallels to Genesis and its discussion by all the major characters as well as the author himself, the novel's theme is somewhat blurred (168). But I think that in order to better appreciate

Steinbeck's theme, we must examine the novel from an Eastern perspective, particularly a Taoist perspective, an angle which the Chinese
character Lee has provided.

Sadly, many early critics consider *East of Eden* a literary disaster,
blaming Steinbeck for not understanding the biblical story and the
American experience. They believe the story of Adam to be the story
of the fall of mankind. But *East of Eden* is not a story of this; it is
a story of the *rise* of mankind. Contrary to the teaching in the Old
Testament, the narrator points out through the voices of Lee and
Samuel—one with an Eastern mind and the other with a Western
mind—that the sixteen verses from Genesis are valuable because
they are a true story of "a history of humankind in any age or culture
or race" (303).

In carrying out his Taoist themes for the novel, Steinbeck created
Lee as his spokesperson. Steinbeck needed Lee's eye because it is non-
Western, and therefore more detached. As Steinbeck emphasized in
Journal of the Novel, he needs a Chinese philosophy, one that is differ-
ent from his western viewpoint.

> Now you are going to like Lee. He is a philosopher. And also he is a kind
> and thoughtful man. And beyond all this he is going to go in the book
> because I need him. The book needs his eye and his criticism which is
> more detached than mine. (73)

In creating such a "foreign" or Eastern character, Steinbeck has Lee
talk pidgin English, wear a queue and Chinese clothes, smoke a Chinese pipe, and drink ng-ka-py. Lee's uniqueness seems to remind the
reader constantly that he is speaking a different language with a different mindset. Steinbeck told Covici that he needed Lee in the story,
"not only as an interpreter, but as an active figure" (149). In the novel,
Lee and his "ancient relatives"—the elderly Chinese, with their dedi-
cated perfectionist study of Hebrew—illustrate differences between
the East and the West that are communicable and dissolvable.

Lee's reasoning sheds some new and different light on this Irish-
American's spiritual life. Samuel had already read quite a lot about
China; now, with Lee's influence, his mind is more inclined toward an
Oriental philosophy (162). At one point, Lee teases him, saying, "And
what do you think of my Oriental pattern, Mr. Hamilton? You know I
am no more Oriental than you are" (271). Here, no matter whether it
is Lee or Samuel indicated in the text, it is in truth Steinbeck who has
been an "Oriental," or one who has cultivated an Oriental mind. Lee's

idea motivated Samuel to make the choice to awaken and enlighten Adam. As for Lee's influence upon his tormented mind, Samuel Hamilton was fully aware of the power in Lee's Eastern thoughts. As he told Adam, "I wonder whether you know what you have in Lee. A philosopher who can cook, or a cook who can think? He has taught me a great deal" (300). Samuel is thus enlightened by the Chinese:

> "It was your two-word retranslation, Lee—'Thou mayest.' It took me by the throat and shook me. And when the dizziness was over, a path was open, new and bright. And my life which is ending seems to be going on to an ending wonderful. And my music has a new last melody like a bird song in the night." (308)

Steinbeck's re-writing of the biblical story makes the human immortal and God-like with power and soul ebbing and flowing like the *Tao* of the cosmos; the writer has dignified human existence vis-à-vis deity and glorified human experience, be it laudable or lamentable. Indeed, as John Ditsky has pointed out, Steinbeck uses Lee "as a challenge to stereotype thinking of all sorts" (49).

Ditsky and several other critics have recently argued that Cal represents the "battle ground between good and evil" (*Steinbeck Newsletter* 9). Cal's capacity to endure this battle demonstrates the Taoist *ying* and *yang* in the story, because "without the capacity for evil, the capacity for good is meaningless" (Ditsky 9). Expanding this argument, we may say that society has become a battleground for the many choices between right and wrong; the human species has become one entity which has to make the right choice in order to survive; the individual soul has to face the torture of the many dilemmas it is handed by nature and by life, in order to function both as a natural being and as a social and rational being. In *The Winter of Our Discontent*, Ethan Allen Hawley's excruciating search for the balance between his natural desires and moral responsibilities is just another example of such a dilemma.

Now let us apply an Eastern mindset to our first category of the paradoxes in *To a God Unknown* and *Burning Bright*. To most western readers, the pagan practices of Joseph Wayne are ridiculous—they are all false—products of a bygone age of human knowledge, such as that of the Native Americans whose cultural origin, some scholars argue, stems from Eastern culture. But this denial of paganism does not make it disappear from human society. Although some branches of Christianity dismiss all other worldviews, Steinbeck must have thought differently; a harmonious world would require a global mindset recognizing religious as well as secular worldviews because "all religions and worldviews are in the heart dialectically related to one another" (Smart 103). Oftentimes, divergent lifestyles and values as well as theories of the human condition obscure the fundamental purpose of humanity as a whole, which is survival for posterity. Steinbeck makes this clear at the end of *Burning Bright* when Joe Saul realizes that the child's blood is his own despite the fact that he is not the father of the child, and he learns to believe that a man is the father of all children. With this view of humankind, Steinbeck developed a scientific worldview which transcends the paradox of "moral" and "immoral" and those of the "Christian way" or the "Devil's way." This solution coincides with the Taoist and Shinto reverence for nature and natural objects.

In *Cannery Row* the paradox is between the contrarieties of war and peace: Cannery Row's informing spirit is an alternative set of human values, devoid of constant fighting, as typified by World War II. *Cannery Row* provides an anecdote that may serve as a panacea for the modern world's inveterate belief in force and struggle for power. In *Cannery Row*, Steinbeck suggests that Lee Chong is "more than a Chinese grocer. He must be. Perhaps he is evil balanced and held suspended by good—an Asian planet held to its orbit by the pull of Lao-Tze and held away from Lao-Tze" (17). Lee's existence and appearance in the novel remind readers of the "otherness" in "us"—humankind. Also in *Cannery Row*, Steinbeck breaks the racial impasse to illustrate the possibilities for communication between races, forming what John Ditsky and Warren French have called a "global village." Ditsky has pointed out such a wonderful example from *Cannery Row* in the character Andy, whom he calls "an idealized version of a very young Steinbeck who may have, at such an age, learned a very useful lesson about people." The lesson Steinbeck, or rather Andy, learned is that people are different, "yet not that different at all" ("The Capacity for Peace" 183).

But at the same time, Steinbeck believes that human beings are not just cultural or political or economic animals, but fundamentally a species in nature, a unique and hopeful part of the whole and never detached totally from it. He writes: "Why do we dread to think of ourselves as a species? Can it be that we are afraid of what we may find? That human self-love would suffer too much and that the image of God might prove to be a mask" (*Sea of Cortez*, 314)? For Steinbeck, the human is neither an animal of low species, nor a super kind, as implied when the term "civilization" crowns us. Steinbeck's work, when placed within the concept of frontier and culture, provides a new perspective of the definitions of those terms. More importantly, this cultural frontier of wholeness and connections to both nature and other human beings is still open, not only for Americans but also for humanity.

NOTE

1. For further discussion, see *Wilderness and the American Mind* by Roderick Nash. New Haven: Yale University Press, 1967.

WORKS CITED

Adams, Hazard, ed. *Critical Theory since Plato*. New York: Harcourt Brace Jo-vanovich, Inc., 1992.

Ames, Roger T. and David L. Hall. *Daodejing: Making This Life Significant*. New York: Ballantine Books, 2003.

Anderson, Norman, ed. *The World's Religions*. Grand Rapids, MI. Eerdman's Publications, 1983.

Astro, Richard. *John Steinbeck and Edward F. Ricketts: The Shaping of a Novelist*. Minneapolis: University of Minnesota Press, 1973.

Benson, Jackson, ed. *The Short Novels of John Steinbeck: Critical Essays with a Checklist to Steinbeck Criticism*. Durham: Duke University Press, 1990.

Campbell, Joseph. *The Masks of God: Oriental Mythology*. New York: Penguin Books, 1991.

Carmody, Denise Lardner and John Tully Carmody. *Eastern Ways to the Center: An Introduction to Asian Religions*. Belmont, CA: Wadsworth Publishing Company, 1983.

Davis, Robert Murray, ed. *Steinbeck: A Collection of Critical Essays*. Englewood Cliffs, NJ: Prentice-Hall, Inc., 1972.

DeMott, Robert. "'Of Ink and Heart's Blood': Episodes in Reading Steinbeck's *East of Eden*." George, 121–31.

Ditsky, John. *Essays on East of Eden*. Steinbeck Monograph Series, No. 7. Muncie, IN: Ball State University, 1977.

———. "'I Kind of Like Caleb': Naming in East of Eden." *The Steinbeck Newsletter* 10(1997): 7–9.

——. *John Steinbeck and His Critics*. Rochester, NY: Camden House, 2000.

——. "'The Capacity for Peace—The Culmination of All the Others': The Internationalism of John Steinbeck and Narrational Technique." Shillinglaw, 171–88.

French, Warren. *John Steinbeck's Fiction Revisited*. New York: Twayne Publishers, 1994.

George, Stephen, ed. *John Steinbeck: A Centennial Tribute*. Westport, CT: Praeger, 2002.

Heavilin, Barbara. "Steinbeck's Spirituality: A Sense of the Ending." George, 93–98.

Lao Tze. *The Wisdom of Laotze*. Trans. Yutang Lin. New York: Random House, Inc., 1948.

Levant, Howard. *The Novels of John Steinbeck: A Critical Study*. Columbia: University of Missouri Press, 1974.

Lewis, R. W. B. "John Steinbeck: The Fitful Daemon." Davis, 163–75.

Li, Luchen. "John Steinbeck's Philosophy Unsettled: East and West: A Mind of the East and the West." *John Stenbeck's Global Dimensions*. Lanham, MD: The Scarecrow Press. 2008: 3-13.

Lisca, Peter. *John Steinbeck: Nature and Myth*. New York: Thomas Y. Crowell, 1978.

Marks, Lester J. *Thematic Design in the Novels of John Steinbeck*. Paris: Mouton, The Hague, 1969.

Meyer, Michael. "Living In (tension) ally: Steinbeck's The Log from the Sea of Cortez as a Reflection of the Balance Advocated in Lao Tze's Tao Teh Ching." Shillinglaw and Hearle, 117–29.

Railsback, Brian. "An Elegant Universe on *Cannery Row*." Shillinglaw and Hearle, 277–294.

Shillinglaw, Susan and Kevin Hearle, eds. *Beyond Boundaries: Rereading John Steinbeck*. Tuscaloosa: The University of Alabama Press, 2002.

Steinbeck, Elaine and Robert Wallsten, eds. *Steinbeck: A Life in Letters*. New York: Penguin Books, 1989.

Steinbeck, John. *East of Eden*. 1952. New York: Penguin Books, 1992.

——. *To a God Unknown*. 1933. New York: Penguin Books, 1995.

——. *Burning Bright*. 1950. New York: Penguin Books, 1995.

——. *Cannery Row*. 1945. New York: Penguin Books, 1994.

——. *Journal of a Novel: The* East of Eden *Letters*. 1952. New York: Penguin Books, 1990.

——. *The Log from the Sea of Cortez*. 1951. New York: Penguin Books, 1995.

——. *America and Americans and Selected Nonfiction*. Ed. Susan Shillinglaw and Jackson J. Benson. New York: Viking, 2002.

Timmerman, John. "John Steinbeck: An Ethics of Fiction." George, 99–106.

12

It's All in Your Head

Transforming Heavenly and Hellish Settings in Steinbeck's *The Pastures of Heaven*

Michael J. Meyer
DePaul and Northeastern Illinois Universities

> Grown old in Love from Seven till Seven times Seven
> I oft have wished for Hell for Ease from Heaven.
>
> —William Blake[1]

That John Steinbeck was a voracious reader and that he often incorporated what he learned from fiction and non-fiction alike into his own canon has been firmly established by Robert DeMott in *Steinbeck's Reading*:

> Steinbeck's prevalent reputation as the impersonal, objective reporter of striking farm workers and dispossessed migrants or as escapist popularizer of primitive views has obscured the roots of his intellectual background, literary interests and artistic methods. He was an author who read to write and who frequently depended on various kinds of documents to supply, augment, or temper his apprehension of reality. . . . The world of books provided Steinbeck with imaginative enrichment, intellectual sustenance and practical resources. (xix)

Writing to his friend Ben Abrahamson in February 1936, Steinbeck confirmed the importance of the causal relationship between reading and his production of art. In the same letter, he lists several works that he considered "realer than [personal] experience, including

Doestoyevsky's *Crime and Punishment,* Flaubert's *Madame Bovary,* Hardy's *The Return of The Native* and "certain" parts of John Milton's *Paradise Lost* (Lisca, *Wide World,* 23). Discovery of the impact of the first three titles on Steinbeck's work has yet to be determined. However, the inclusion of the last title is not surprising since Steinbeck was clearly immersed in Milton's great epic during the composition of *In Dubious Battle,* his fifth novel (see letter to George Albee, January 15, 1935, Steinbeck and Wallsten 99).

Two other letters to friends also clearly establish the author's debt to Milton and the intentional interconnectedness between the two texts. "It [my new novel] is called *Dubious Battle* from the lines in the first part of the argument of *Paradise Lost,*" he writes to George Archer on 15 January 1933 (Steinbeck and Wallsten 99). Later still, his correspondence with Wilbur Needham in 1936 reiterates: "My new book is called *In Dubious Battle* after the magnificent passage in the beginning of *Paradise Lost* where Lucifer speaks of 'the innumerable force of spirits armed'" (letter housed in Clifton Barrett Library, University of Virginia).

Numerous critics have expounded on the appropriateness of the title for Steinbeck's fifth novel and the impact of Milton on Steinbeck's stylistics as well as his themes. (See Hayashi, 98; Fontenrose, 44–53: Lisca, *Nature and Myth,* 71–76; Timmerman, 81–88; and French, 69–70). Few, however, have suggested a similar Miltonic influence on *The Pastures of Heaven,* Steinbeck's work which appeared six years before *In Dubious Battle;* nor has anyone cited a specific passage from the epic which may have influenced the composition of Steinbeck's short story cycle.

Although the author's ironic depiction of a potential Eden in *Pastures* has been explored extensively, no critic has yet speculated that the false appearances of the lush valley known as The Corral de Cielo offers a clear parallel to the solution Satan provides his evil cohorts as he discovers himself in Hell after being expelled from Paradise for an unsuccessful rebellion against God the Father. In Book I of *Paradise Lost,* Satan suggests the construction of a rival city in Hell that will offer competition to the glories of Heaven, the uncorrupted throne of the Deity. This carefully planned temporal palace (appropriately named Pandemonium) suggests that Satan and the lesser devils use confusion and panic as building materials as they try to re-form a fiery pit into a kingdom that they hope even God himself might envy.

*   *   *

Although Milton notes that the materials used in the construction include "ribs of gold" dug from the hills of Hell, he also suggests that the elements are in reality base metals merely transformed by alchemy to have the appearance of richness and elegance. The outward appearance of wealth and beauty is mere trickery and deception. In addition, since Pandemonium is so quickly erected also indicates its lack of quality. Milton's word choice reaffirms such a conclusion by combining the "wondrous art" (read artifice) of the city's buildings with the words "*scummed* the bullion *dross*" (emphasis added). Thus the author employs a vocabulary which suggests the inferiority of the construction materials rather than an edifice that has an innate ability to rival Paradise.

In Book I, Milton compares Pandemonium with the pagan cities of Alcairo (Cairo in Egypt) and Babylon in Syria, cities whose wealth and bounty were extensive and renowned, but whose reliance on material wealth acquired by human beings rather than on the blessings of the Deity eventually led to their destruction. The key lines in *Paradise Lost*, Book I that surely influenced Steinbeck, however, occur far earlier than the creation of Pandemonium, beginning at line 242 where Satan exclaims:

> Is this the region, this the clime
> Said the lost Archangel, this the seat
> That we must change for Heaven, this mournful gloom
> For that celestial light. . . .
> Farewell happy fields
> Where joy forever dwells, hail horrors, hail
> Infernal world, and thou profoundest Hell
> Receive thy new Possessor who brings
> A mind not to be chang'd by place or time.
> The mind is its own place and in itself
> Can make a Heav'n of Hell, a Hell of Heav'n.

In these oft-quoted lines from Milton's epic, Satan determines to cope with being thrust from the glory of his former home. He will intellectually create a new one, using his mental power to deny loss and to re-create and reshape reality and truth into facts more compatible to his interpretation.

Perhaps Milton's ideas here even predate *Paradise Lost* and are de-
rivatives of Shakespeare's *Hamlet*, where the prince, in a discussion
with his college friends Rosencrantz and Guildenstern, comments on
his perception of Denmark as a prison. When Rosencrantz and Guildenstern disagree, Hamlet replies, "For there is nothing either bad or
good but thinking makes it so. To me it is a prison" (*Hamlet*, Act II,
sc. 3, ll. 252–53).[2]

Further support of Steinbeck's intent to mirror a fallen world in
Pastures of Heaven, a world peopled by flawed personalities intent on
regaining Paradise, is provided in Steinbeck's letter to Amasa "Ted"
Miller in 1931, provided by his biographer, Jackson J. Benson:

> I am doing a thing called *The Pastures of Heaven* which takes the name
> from an enclosed valley in the mountains named by the Spanish dis-
> coverer Las Pasturas de Cielo. . . . The plan is simple and strangely
> enough true. . . . I am simply taking a number of families and show-
> ing the influence of unconscious evil. . . . You see each separate family
> will be a separate narrative with its own climax and end and they will
> be joined by locality, by the same characters entering into each and by
> this nameless sense and power of evil. . . . I think the ironic name *The
> Pastures of Heaven* and the nebulous parallel of the M _____s with a
> Miltonian Lucifer is fairly good. It would make a very readable book I
> think. (210–11)

Moreover, Benson's earlier revelations that at the same time Steinbeck
had been reading Carl Jung, "thinking about the black depths of people" (206), reading the Bible a great deal, and underlining passages
in the Old Testament lend credence to the contention that a complex
combination of literary resources influenced the development of
Pastures. Nevertheless, the Miltonian/Shakespearean allusions mentioned above remain relatively unexplored.

Despite their brief nature, I believe references to these interrelated
sources are employed frequently in the text, with each repeating allusion used in a variety of ways in the individual stories. By invoking
Milton's lines about the power of the human mind to transform all
things, I believe Steinbeck tries to make an equal division of characters in his novel. Some attempt to make a heaven of their personal
hells while others, both consciously and unconsciously, transform
their Edenic gardens into devilish places. The former group includes
Tuleracito, Molly Morgan, the Lopez sisters, and Pat Humbert, while

the latter encompasses Helen Van de Venter, Burt Munroe, Raymond Banks, and Junius Maltby.

All members of the first group suffer from loneliness and rejection, and they all use their intellects to transform their worlds into locations that are more compatible and congenial—places of acceptance, care, and concern that will soothe their battered egos. For example, both Tuleracito and Molly Morgan replace real worlds that threaten them with fictional ones that have more appeal.

Tuleracito, for instance, initially uses his artistic talent to combat people's false perception that labels him as animal-like, troglodytic, and a malignant presence in the community. Steinbeck's narrator describes his sandstone carvings of animals in great detail, suggesting Tuleracito's talent and the perfection of his craft; however, he also notes that the community considers his skill to be "diabolical." (49) In school, when his artwork is erased, Tuleracito flies into an almost maniacal rage, angered that his "reality" has been unappreciated and even destroyed by his classmates After this incident, he becomes even more isolated, and his world turns ever bleaker and more hellish.

When a new teacher arrives, Tuleracito finds yet another way besides art to make a heaven of his hell. This occurs through the fantasy tales Miss Morgan shares with her class. According to Steinbeck, as Miss Morgan reads about "elves, brownies, fairies, pixies, and changelings, [Tuleracito's] interest centered and [he] leaned toward the teacher to intercept her words" (56). Eventually, these fantasy tales become so real in Tuleracito's mind that he begins to believe he is a descendent of gnomes, a culture in which he hopes to find a niche of acceptance and similarity, unlike his present reality.

As he digs in the Munroe's property in search of his "relatives," Tuleracito attempts to reshape reality into a more acceptable form. His new perception of "truth" helps him to identify with a new community, one that neither ridicules him nor tries to make him conform to what is "normal." His oddities and strange disposition are no longer unusual in a world of his own making. Unfortunately, his search for a "heaven" where he will be accepted and finally belong is interrupted by the meddlesome Bert Munroe. Ultimately misunderstood and thwarted in his search for a better place, Tuleracito is not only physically subdued but is also eventually relegated to an asylum for the criminally insane as a result of his violent attempt to pursue his new world. One can only guess that even though he is incarcerated, his mind will continue to struggle in an attempt to conquer and over-come the even greater hell he now faces.

Molly Morgan, the school teacher, follows a pattern similar to Tu-leracito. Although she is an accepted member of society, unlike the Little Frog, she too suffers from low self-esteem. In the flashbacks of Molly's childhood, she remembers her youth, complete with the "old squalid unpainted house" (135) in which she grew up. Described as miserable and poor, Molly reveals her relationship with her mother in italicized passages and relates how she conquered her sorrows and depression by listening to the adventure stories her vagabond father told during his infrequent returns to the family residence. Like the fantasy stories she shares with Tuleracito, these stories, "cities and people, strange people; always adventures, and a hundred funny inci-dent," (138) always seem to mitigate the hellish existence that Molly faces daily in her youth and adolescence.

Later, with her mother dead and her father chronically absent from her life, Molly's self-esteem is further harmed by an agreement to work as a servant for a Mrs. Morris, at whose home she is constantly nagged and criticized as inferior and described as "not worth a cent." (142). Molly counters this hellish existence by dreaming about her father, emphasizing the excitement of foreign places and exciting events. Dressed finely in a cutaway coat, striped trousers and a top hat and carrying red roses, Molly's father is depicted as a man who will whisk his daughter off to exotic places and who will ultimately res-cue her from a mundane existence. In addition, Molly envisions him as similar to the Mexican desperado Vasquez, who is considered an adventurer and heroic figure. Romanticizing this foreign-born "hero" as similar to her constantly moving father, Molly is able to envision Vasquez's rundown cabin on a local hillside as far different from its crass reality. Though the literal remains are described as "rotting wooden walls and the dehydrated smell of the earth," (147), to Molly the surroundings become a lush valley hilltop whose "orchards lay in dark green squares; the grass was yellow and the hills behind a light brown washed with lavender" (148). She also imagines Vasquez and her father with elegant clothing and happy dispositions as she turns the negatives of her real life into fantastical and fictional positives.

Ultimately motivated by a fear that her self-created illusion will soon dissolve or dissipate and that the drunken cow-hand at the Munroe place may turn out to be her true father, Molly decides to leave Las Pasturas before the "reality" she has so carefully constructed in her mind is shattered. Instead, Molly chooses to retreat from the idyllic valley created by her imagination and to return to a world of loneliness and self-doubt that had dominated her life in the past. Her heavenly environs are revealed as difficult to maintain, and she discovers the difficulty of single-handedly inventing positive surroundings to replace negative ones. Eventually she is forced to admit that her father is more like the actual Vasquez than the gallant bandelero she has created in her fantasies. This real Vasquez is described by Bill Whiteside as a "common thief" (149), and the fear of encountering such a reality causes Molly to leave Las Pasturas abruptly in search of a home where her past may not intrude so rudely on the fantasies that keep her afloat.

Like Miss Morgan and Tuleracito, the Lopez sisters depicted in Chapter 7 of *Pastures* have similar coping mechanisms for their drab existence. Their farm is described in the first paragraph as strangely unproductive for the lush valley. It is "40 acres of rocky hillside" and "practically nothing would grow on the starved soil except tumbleweed and flowering sage and, although the sisters toiled mightily over a little garden, they succeeded in producing very few vegetables" (*POH* 115).

Faced with poverty after the death of their father, Maria and Rosa idealistically concoct a plan to change their negatives into positives. First they transform the outside of their homestead with whitewash and geranium cuttings, assuming that a shift in outward appearances will provide even more customers for their budding restaurant business. When they discover that the sale of food improves even more when accompanied by the "gift" of flesh which follows its consumption, both Rosa and Maria rationalize their sexual looseness, transforming the act of prostitution into a positive by thinking of the act of intercourse not as a grievous sin but as a way to impart happiness and joy into the lives of others. As Milton's Satan contended, the event is transformed by how the Lopez sisters perceive it.

As a result of their changed perception of their environs, Steinbeck inserts a description of the sisters' surroundings that is far more desirable than his initial picture of their home. Steinbeck writes: "The hills glistened with dew. Maria sang more loudly. . . . A meadow lark flew ahead from post to post, singing loudly" (123). But once again, this illusory bubble of Heaven on earth is only temporary, for Rosa

and Maria are fated to return to "the old way with no new dresses"
(128). Threatened with arrest for running a house of ill-repute, the
sisters are literally exiled from Las Pasturas; given no other options,
they decide to move to San Francisco and become "bad" women in
earnest. One wonders how long it will take them to rationalize life
in the city bordello as they did when they ran the restaurant on their
own rural property and sold sexual favors along with their Mexican
dishes. If they can transform evil to good once, surely they are capable
of repeating the feat again and again.

Finally, the tale of Pat Humbert provides Steinbeck's most extensive
study of the human ability to create a heaven out of hell. As Steinbeck
notes, "All of Pat's life had been spent in an atmosphere of age, of the
aches and illness, of the complaints and self sufficiency of age" (177).
Even as a child, he is beset with the pessimism and depression of his
elderly parents; relegated to hard work in order to provide constant
care for individuals who are more critical than appreciative, his youth
is filled with bitterness and resentment.

His physical surroundings are also hellish, mirroring the attitudes
of his parents. The Humbert homestead is "an old rambling farm-
house of five rooms, a locked parlor, cold and awful as doom, a
hot stuffy sitting room smelling always of pungent salve and patent
medicines, two bedrooms and a large kitchen" (178). Only when
lengthy illnesses claim the lives of both parents can Pat begin to
think of changing his lifestyle, but even then he hesitates to begin
any transformation. The parlor especially becomes a symbol of the
terrible hold that death, illness, and the past have on this thirty-year
old. Steinbeck describes closed blinds, oppressing religious symbols,
photos and pictures: "So cold and sepulchral was this parlor that it
had never been entered except by corpses and their attendants. It was
indeed a little private mortuary chamber" (179). Replete with stuffed
birds and a portrait of the Arthurian Elaine draped in a gray shroud,
the room is a domineering force in Pat's empty existence, chaining
him to a somber and depressing past.

Steinbeck's depiction of setting in this chapter are among his best,
rivaling the sections of *The Grapes of Wrath* that so vividly portray the
sights and sounds of the Dust Bowl in the mid-thirties. For example,
on his return from the burial of his parents, Pat's tactile sense is as-
saulted by a wave of cold, lifeless air in the house. Similarly, his nos-
trils are assailed by the smell of funeral flowers and age and medicine.
(183). Finding his whole being invaded by the negativity of the parlor

and the misery it reminds him of, Pat decides to avoid that particular room in the future, locking it and throwing away the key in hopes of locking up "the two thin old ghosts," but he is ultimately unable to take "away their power to trouble him" (185).

Humbert's denial of the house's control over him is further illustrated in his extensive absences from it and his attempts to find joy in the homes and activities of the other residents of Las Pasturas. As a result, the old building is "moldering with neglect," the only sign of life being a white Banksia rose that suddenly springs to life and eventually initiates a new attitude and a new beginning for Humbert. Steinbeck describes the rose as follows: "It covered the porch, hung festoons over the closed windows and dropped long streamers from the eaves. People passing by on the county road paused to marvel at its size and beauty" (189).

Initially, however, Humbert invests himself in his farmland, barely noticing the enormous change that has begun to transform the house. It is almost as if he prefers to forget the dreary building he must return to every evening and replace it with dreams of potentially fertile ground that will help him overcome his depression. Ultimately, his neighbor Mae Munroe's reaction to this rose motivates Humbert to begin the transformation of the inside of the house so that its beauty will rival that of the rose. His goal is to create an interior that will mirror the elegant Vermont house that Mae envisions in her mind.

Soon he realizes that changing the bleak rooms inside the dwelling is indeed feasible, and he imagines that such a change could please the impressionable and beautiful young Miss Munroe as well. As Pat's mind awakens to the possibilities, he initiates plans for arrangement, color, and line. Soon his mental construct of a heavenly place where he can spend his future with Mae emerges. Moreover, he becomes determined that the loneliness and decay he presently experiences daily will slowly disappear. Like Satan's Pandemonium, the house begins as a potential reality, a temporary positive that has the potential to emerge from totally negative surroundings.

Humbert's first move is to break the lock to the parlor and to attack the hated and ancient room with renewed vigor. Next he strips the whole room of its furnishings, burning them in the back yard and washing the interior walls with buckets of cleansing water. He is so intent on destroying the ugliness that has controlled him for so long that the creation of a place of beauty comes almost too naturally. Again Steinbeck devotes a great deal of space to his description of the setting, concentrating on Pat's redecorating scheme that replaces cold and darkness with warmth and light.

Yet when the redecorating is completed and the house remade, it should not be surprising that Humbert is no more fortunate than his neighbors. The Miltonic Satan's assumption that positive thoughts are all powerful is once again shown as a fragile solution. Although the mind may momentarily create an illusion that evil can be transformed into good just by thinking, the concept is rudely shattered when Pat's dream of marriage with Mae Munroe and a positive future in his Edenic house disappears with Mae's announcement of her engagement to Bill Whiteside. Thus discouragement and failure occur despite the intensive redecorating and remodeling, and again "the rambling house was dark and unutterably dreary" (201) when Pat returns in disappointment after the revelation. Steinbeck suggests that he may choose to live in the barn rather than confront the spoiled transformation and the broken dream.

Through these episodes, Steinbeck implies there will be a time of realization similar to Satan's in *Paradise Lost*, when the faulty logic like that employed by Satan will be seen for what it is—a clever trick that momentarily allows a naïve human being (as well as the evil angels) to believe in his own mortal power and ability to overcome a heavenly decree with mere earthly effort. Clearly, such is not the case.

While the rationalization evident in the first four characters may make it seem that it is relatively easy to transform hell into heaven, readers might expect the alternative—making heaven into hell—to be far more difficult. Given the human penchant for evil and destruction, however, the task becomes relatively simple. One has only to look at Milton's Satan to observe how easy it becomes for an individual to rationalize that Paradise must be an inferior place. Arguing his lack of freedom, Satan finds Paradise lacking because there he cannot lead—a lack, he feels, that reduces him to a servile, second-rate position. Therefore, it is no wonder that this leader of darkness says, "Better to reign in hell than serve in Heav'n" (*Paradise Lost*, Book I, l. 263) or that his goal becomes to thwart the Almighty's power:

> If then his Providence
> Out of our evil seek to bring forth good,
> Our labor must be to pervert that end,
> And out of good still to find means of evil.

> —*Paradise Lost*, Book I, ll. 161–64

Thus the heaven-into-hell stories are neatly balanced with the hell-into-heaven tales that include the histories of Las Pasturas residents Helen Van de Venter, Shark Wicks, Raymond Banks, and Junius Maltby.

The reader meets Mrs. Van de Venter shortly after the death of her husband, Hubert, and the birth of her child, Hilda. In the beginning, Hilda's surroundings are described as littered with death, a situation represented by her husband's big game trophies that decorate the walls of her home. The heads of game animals infect the environs with darkness and depression, and Helen herself seems prone to exulting in tragedy. In addition, she is beset by the predisposition of her only daughter to violence and mental illness. Largely in an attempt to isolate herself from the intrusion of an outside world, Helen decides to move to Las Pasturas and Christmas Canyon, an area of superb beauty that might be expected to challenge and compete with her former pessimistic lifestyle. As the story progresses, however, it is evident that even the most beautiful setting can be transformed into a dark and foreboding place.

Despite the perfection of the log house and the lovely landscaping of trees and colorful flowers, Helen remains predisposed to a tragic existence, and Steinbeck emphasizes her attraction by calling attention to her "love of the hair-shirt" (70–72). Thus, despite the perfection of her new surroundings, Helen continues to hunger "for tragedy," and Steinbeck informs his readers that "life had lavishly heaped it upon her" (64). Very soon the hellish nature of her daughter's illness invades the pristine beauty of her new home, and it becomes evident that Helen will no longer be able to hide Hilda away, even in a lavish and harmonic setting.

Ironically, although Helen's new home has a "delicious peacefulness," Hilda's reaction is just the opposite, and she becomes determined to escape from what she perceives as an "old house," not a spacious and lovely home (79, 81). In contrast, Helen dreams of a potential paradise:

> Helen glanced out her window. The dusk was coming already from the hilltops. Already a few bats looped nervously about. The quail were calling out to one another as they went to water, and far down the canyon, the cows were lowing on their way in toward the milking sheds. A change was stealing over Helen. She was filled with a new sense of peace; she felt protected and clothed against the tragedies that had beset her for so long. She stretched her arms outward and forward, and sighed comfortably. (78)

Once again Steinbeck emphasizes the mind's power, for to Helen the new place is "infested with life . . . just bursting with life" (83) while to Hilda it remains a restrictive and repressive setting designed to curb her freedom. As Helen struggles to dismiss the tragic past and her husband's predisposition to death and destruction, Steinbeck portrays her as potentially successful, for to her

> the room looked different and felt different. She fumbled with the new window bolts and threw wide the windows to the night. And the night wind sighed in and bathed her bare shoulders with its cool peace. She leaned out the window and listened. (81)

Yet ultimately, such idealism is futile. The two conflicting views of Christmas Canyon must be resolved; unfortunately, this resolution occurs with Hilda's death after she escapes her barred room in an attempt to run away with a potential "prince-charming/rescuer."

Since Hilda is presumably murdered by her own mother in an attempt to end the violence her mental condition might foster, the event serves as an indicator of Helen's recognition of the futility of trying to maintain a positive attitude about change in the face of so great odds. The potential for renewal lost, Helen returns to her earlier predisposition, welcoming fate's tragic hand in her life. A hell of suffering returns to dominate her future as Helen confesses to Dr. Phillips that "I know what my life expects of me" (84). The implied answer is, of course, a continuing lack of happiness and joy.

Using a similar technique in the episode about the Battle farm, Steinbeck tells his readers that the farm was not originally thought of as a hellish or cursed place, but as a "poem" of cultivated and carefully tended beauty:

> The trees in the orchards were trimmed and groomed. The vegetables grew, crisp and green in their line-straight rows. George [Battle] cared for his house and kept a flower garden in front of it. . . . The farm was a poem by the inarticulate man. (6–7)

Yet the Battle place is unable to maintain its pristine appearance, for as its owners experience "curses" rather than "blessings," the area develops into a "weedy blot between two finely cultivated, contented pieces of land" (5).

As time passes and new owners arrive, the farm deteriorates and falls prey to harmful elements rather than realizing its Edenic potential:

The weeds, with holiday energy free of fear of the hoe, grew as large as small trees. In the orchard, the fruit trees were knotty and strong and tangled. They increased the quantity of their fruit and diminished its size. The brambles grew about their roots and swallowed up the windfalls. . . . There was something fearful about the gaunt old house with its staring vacant windows. The white paint fell off in long scales; the shingles curled up shaggily, the farm itself went completely wild. (4; 8–9)

This deterioration begins to occur five years after disaster meets the second generation of the Battles and results in the death of George Battle's son John from the bite of a rattlesnake. The curse on the land seems so strong that even an attempt by the Mustrovics, the new owners, to restore the former glow to the land fails, for although the land revives, the house is still neglected—unpainted, with broken windows with flypaper stretched over them to keep out the air (10).

When the Mustrovics mysteriously disappear, the neighbors proclaim, "It's good land but I wouldn't own it if you gave it to me. . . . There's something funny about the place, almost creepy" (11). Only the arrival of a new mindset in the form of the middle-class value system espoused by Bert Monroe offers the farm some potential for restoration. As easily as heaven became hell under the former owners, it returns to its former state under the work ethic of the fastidious Munroe family. Once again Steinbeck asserts the capabilities of the human mind to decree what will be so and to return the land to positive environs.

Raymond Banks provides a third example of an individual who constructs a hell out of heaven. Banks's house in Las Pasturas is described in idyllic detail, with his whitewashed residence "set on the edge of a grove of oak trees," with "many flowers around it, . . . calendulas and big African marigolds and cosmos and asters as high as trees, . . . and a rose garden worthy the name in the valley of the Pastures of Heaven." Residing on a model farm in the valley, his home is also known as both "immaculate and new," with a "great flock of clean white chickens eating and scratching on green alfalfa. Finer still were the thousand white ducks sailing magnificently on the pond" (155–56).

Yet despite his heavenly location and lovely home, Banks revels in death, similar to Hubert Van de Venter's passion for killing animals. For example, he exults in the killing of his young roosters and, in a deliberate parallel, has a bizarre infatuation with attending executions at the local prison. In appearance, Raymond's healthy and hearty demeanor also seems "incongruous and strangely obscene" to his neighbors (163). The paradox of his outwardly positive good nature and his love for children also appears unseemly to the narrator.

Like Helen, Raymond is another character who seems comfortable with the contradictions that arise with his preference for death over life, negatives over positives. Although Banks's mind is able to rationalize his actions, his encounters with Bert Munroe surprisingly suggest that his preoccupation with death is far from normal, perhaps even somewhat sadistic. Munroe causes Banks to realize that his fascination with hangings is repulsive rather than admirable. Again, it is the perspective of a different human mind which turns Banks's supposedly positive life into a depressing negative from which he will find it hard to recover. Despite the beautiful outward appearance of his farm, Banks discovers an emptiness in his existence, a feeling of loneliness and rejection. The evil intent that he originally believed was a tolerable choice now surfaces and haunts him, causing him to cancel his regular trip to the executions and to reevaluate his actions.

A final example of a character whose heaven is changed into hell is Junius Maltby. Having escaped from the drudgery of life as an accountant in San Francisco and moved to Las Pasturas for health reasons, Junius finds that his new surroundings do wonders for his physical well-being. His color improves as he breathes fresh air, he gains weight, and his eyesight grows stronger (86).

Shortly thereafter, after marrying and experiencing the death of his wife and stepsons, Junius is left with an only child, Robbie, and the responsibility to raise him. Following a non-conformist agenda, Junius decides that the boy should be brought up in nature—away from the responsibility and demands of "normal" society. He encourages Robbie's full use of leisure time for enjoyment and study, finding most work and toil altogether reprehensible. This "laziness," as it is labeled by his neighbors, accounts for their refusal to accept Maltby and for those Las Pasturas residents devoted to the work ethic—such as Humbert, Munroe, and Banks—to condemn and isolate him.

Since Junius ignores society's demands for acquisition and material wealth, his resistance appears to Steinbeck to be positive, even heavenly, for Junius recognizes that the good life is hardly determined by either money or possessions. Instead, he spends his days in luxurious relaxation, contemplating the glories of the countryside and indulging in reading both delightful and instructive books. Like Tuleracito and Molly Morgan, Junius has discovered the potential for fiction, a construct of the mind, to reshape his surroundings, making what some would label a shabby existence into an ideal life, shorn of obligations and stress.

In a true return to the randomness of nature as opposed to the regulation of human society, Junius procrastinates in planting his crops and then forgets about them—they are "always too late, often forgotten and covered in weeds" (91). The paradisical happiness of Maltby consists of quiet contemplation and erudite conversation rather than an acquisitive desire to attain more and more goods in order to gain the approval of his fellow citizens. By ignoring the human regulation of the natural world, Junius creates a setting that even Thoreau would envy, a place where things are allowed to "be" rather than "forced to be" by other's expectations. Junius and his housemate Jacob Stutz

> didn't make conversation; rather they let a seedling of thought sprout by itself and then watched with wonder while it sent out branching limbs. They didn't direct their thinking or trim it the way so many people do." (93)

This time, however, it is the ideas of the group rather than the individual that conspire to make Junius's earthly paradise demonic.

Unable to cope with Maltby's construct of a world so unlike their own, the residents of Las Pasturas decide to "help" him to see its defects, to view his farm as a place where his son is deprived of "fine" clothes and "competent" schooling and where Junius impedes good rather than fosters it. First, the neighbors criticize the maintenance of his farm, pointing out that his "land was overgrown with weeds and littered with untrimmed fruit trees and fallen fences." They find Junius's failure to maintain his property reprehensible, and the rose-colored glasses through which he has seen an ideal world are fogged and blurred by others' so-called "sharp" vision of reality. Eventually, the neighbors impose such rigid societal norms for Junius that he views his liberal and unfettered lifestyle as evil rather than good, confining rather than free.

Rejecting Junius's game-like attitude towards life, the community advocates the gravity or seriousness of existence. Consequently, since having fun can hardly be an acceptable way to live, only middle-class respectability and morals can be worthy goals. It is no wonder that the intellectual curiosity and the leisure time that Junius used to foster it are ultimately condemned as unnatural and irrelevant to a world where success is measured by acquisition rather than happiness. His self-constructed heavenly retreat is rudely demolished, and Junius reluctantly plans a return to the big city where he will resume his boring job and follow the acquisitive lifestyle he once was fortunate to escape. It is the final portrait of a heaven turned hellish.

Clearly, Steinbeck's organizational pattern suggests that he consciously tried to echo or reiterate the concepts of Milton in *Paradise Lost* and perhaps the ideas of Shakespeare in *Hamlet* as well. In addition, while the body of *Pastures* explores the ironic nature of the residents of Las Pasturas, the novel also draws attention to notable passages in Milton and Shakespeare through the frame stories that serve as bookends to the tales of the single characters that form individual chapters. For example, the Spanish corporal of the preface, the initial discoverer of the lush valley, and the bus passengers of the epilogue, who observe the tranquil area from afar, suggest the author's determination to examine the claim that an individual mind can make a hell of heaven or a heaven of hell. While each intuits the vast potential for good in the Edenic valley named Las Pasturas de Cielo, they also acknowledge that this positive is paradoxically countered by a veiled evil that also dwells there. The fluctuation between these two extremes is dependent on individual attitudes and the beliefs of each resident or observer. It is mind over matter. One has only to note the bus passengers' shifting reactions to Las Pasturas to see that in one minute their reaction to the valley is positive while in practically the next moment, they find it undesirable or inappropriate to meet their needs.

No doubt Steinbeck's attraction to this thematic emphasis was based to a large degree on the fact that he was writing during the onset of The Great Depression. Following the stock market crash on Black Tuesday, October 29, 1929, most Americans had no choice but to rely on the power of their imaginations to dispel the harsh realities of poverty, despair, and loss that dominated their everyday existence. It is noteworthy that in the early thirties the arts in America deliberately tried to foster and mirror America's gritty determination to survive the throes of despair by reshaping reality. In words and music, artists strove to bring hope, a virtue that would enable their audiences to replace the grimness of daily problems with a brighter future.

Perhaps following a pattern set by "Hobo" songs sung by migrant workers down on their luck, Steinbeck chose to present *The Pastures of Heaven* as an elusive Eden, yet one which even the "down-and-out" have the potential to recapture. Like the searchers in "The Big Rock Candy Mountain," a ballad of the time attributed to Harry "Haywire Mac" McClintock, Steinbeck's characters demonstrate the power of imagination to transform the inherent pessimism of the times. The residents of Las Pasturas, like the narrator of the ballad, seek a place where positives outweigh negatives, where ideals flourish and grow. The songwriter envisions

> A lake of gin
> We can both jump in
> Where the handouts grow on bushes
>
> In the new mown hay
> We can sleep all day
> And the bars all have free lunches. (Stanza 2)

McClintock's ballad also envisions a "land of milk and honey" where a bum "won't need no money (Stanza 1). Moreover, the weather is ideal, and "they hang the jerk that invented work" (Stanza 5). Envisioning "cigarette trees" and "lemonade springs where the bluebird sings," the ballad's refrain ends with the depiction of the big rock candy mountain, a "sweet" creation of the mind that eases the sorrow and pain of everyday living.

Although it is unclear whether the ballad was extant before the publication of the novel and thus could also have been an influence on Steinbeck's composition, it is evident that both songwriter and novelist believed in the human ability to make heavens out of hells and hells out of heavens—at least for a moment or two. The theme of the power of the human mind, celebrated by both Milton and Shakepeare, reappears in *The Pastures of Heaven*, as Steinbeck reworks old perceptions and presents them in a new way.

NOTES

1. From [Notebook], "Grown Old" 1; E516 found at the Blake Digital Text Project, http://www.english.uga.edu/Blake_Concondance/.

2. DeMott's listing 730 in *Steinbeck's Reading* indicates that Steinbeck's personal library included the complete works of Shakespeare. Edited by William G. Clark and William A. Wright in 17 volumes printed by John Alden in 1897.

WORKS CITED

Benson, Jackson J. *The True Adventures of John Steinbeck: Writer*. New York: Penguin, 1984.

DeMott, Robert. *Steinbeck's Reading: A Catalogue of Books Owned and Borrowed*. New York: Garland Press, 1984.

Fontenrose, Joseph. *John Steinbeck: An Introduction and Interpretation*. New York: Barnes and Novel, 1969.

French, Warren. *John Steinbeck's Fiction Re-Visited*. New York: Twayne, 1994.

McClintock, Harry. "Haywire Mac." Lyrics to "Big Rock Candy Mountain." http://ingeb.org/songs/onasumme.html

Lisca, Peter. *Nature and Myth*. New York: Thomas Y. Crowell, 1978.

Steinbeck, Elaine and Robert Wallsten, eds. *Steinbeck: A Life in Letters*. New York: Viking, 1984.

Steinbeck, John. *The Pastures of Heaven*. New York: Robert O. Ballou, 1932. Reprinted Penguin Books, 1980.

Timmerman, John. *John Steinbeck's Fiction: The Aesthetics of the Road Taken*. Norman: University of Oklahoma Press, 1986.

13

The Short, Happy Life of *Pippin IV*

The Grand Joke

Brian Railsback
Western Carolina University

In February, 1959, Ernest Hemingway was holed up in Ketchum, Idaho, grieving over the recent burial of his good friend, Taylor Williams. This death and others reminded Hemingway of his own mortality, and he was anxious to pull together as much work as he could in the time he had left. "All these people dying makes me feel I should work harder on account of time is so short," he wrote in a letter to an editor in the trade department at Scribners. Continuing, he wrote concerning his publisher, Charles Scribner, "I hope to have plenty more good books for him. . . . We have plenty of stuff ahead. Some wonderful and I will cut out the shit" (893). He was determined not to let his serious work slip: "I could give him a book every year like Steinbeck composed of my toenail clippings (i.e., reprint of war correspondence), little fantasies about King Poo Poo or author toe jam. But that is all shit and just the byproducts of egotism or avarice or both" (893–94). "King Poo Poo" was, of course, John Steinbeck's 1957 satire, *The Short Reign of Pippin IV*.

Hemingway's private remarks about Steinbeck demonstrated his annoyance with Steinbeck as competition; Ernest was contending, as he once put it in 1940, with "a cloud of Steinbecks" (511). In 1938, he was proud to observe that there was more new material by word count in his short story collection, *The First Forty-Nine*, than there was in Steinbeck's *Of Mice and Men*. Like many of Steinbeck's critics and detractors, Hemingway still grudgingly accepted his competitor as a force to be reckoned with. Despite his disparaging remarks about *The Short Reign of Pippin IV*, in the same year that he wrote them he insisted to his last ingénue, Valerie (Danby-Smith) Hemingway, that Steinbeck was one of the important American authors, whom she should read immediately; and among the books he bought for her was *Pippin*. She also recalled an American in France who saluted Hemingway by exclaiming, "'Mr. Steinbeck, you're my favorite author'" (Valerie Hemmingway 68). What bedeviled Hemingway was how a writer of Steinbeck's stature could write something like "King Poo Poo"; he could only reason that such products were a result of ego or greed.

The Short Reign of Pippin IV irritated Steinbeck's closest allies as well. Both his long-time editor, Pascal Covici, and his literary agent, Elizabeth Otis, wished the author would have worked on something else, something more substantial. In his exhaustive biography of Steinbeck's life, Jackson J. Benson notes that *Pippin* was the only book Viking tried to persuade Steinbeck not to publish and that "both Elizabeth and Pat had come to hate it" (803).

Initially, Steinbeck himself resisted the concept behind *Pippin*, a satire that came to him while he and Elaine Steinbeck stayed at a house in Paris across the street from the Elysee Palace in 1954 (the setting of Pippin's home in the novel). In February 1956 Steinbeck intended to work on an experimental novel, *Pi Root*, but found the idea for *Pippin* kept intruding. "I am constantly amazed and to a certain extent frightened by the vagrant tendency of my mind and writing direction," he wrote to his agent. "It seems so often to take its own direction—can be resisted but goes into a pout if it is resisted" (Benson 784). So he started on what was supposed to be a short story but which was clearly becoming, by March 1956, a novel. "It is the wrong length, the wrong subject and everything else is wrong with it except that it is fun and I could not resist writing it," Steinbeck wrote in a letter to his friend, Webster "Toby" Street, "I must say I do have fun with my profession, if that's what it is" (Steinbeck, *Letters* 524–25). By April he had his first draft but shared his disappointment with it in a letter to Otis: "Attempting to make it a satire on scholarship in addition to everything else, I am afraid I came too close to the thing I was satirizing. It was dull" (Benson 786). Still, he enjoyed the project enough to promise a significant revision in the future. After a stint of summer reporting on the Democratic and Republican national conventions, he tried to get back to work on the *Pippin* manuscript. By the fall some of his original delight in the project had dissipated, Pascal Covici's obvious lack of enthusiasm was vexing, and he spent an unusual length of time (for Steinbeck) reworking the book.

He kept on, however, as a point of rebellion. He felt that Covici wanted him to "write the *Grapes of Wrath* over and over" (Benson 794). His editor might have been pleased to have Steinbeck do what he did to his earlier political satire, "L'Affaire Lettuceberg": burn it. Steinbeck was not going to write as a way to position for the Nobel or other literary prizes, as he felt Faulkner and Hemmingway were doing; "It is almost as though they were fighting for billing on a tombstone," he wrote (Benson 796). Regarding the quest for the Nobel Prize, Steinbeck wrote to Covici's son that the prize "kind of retires" a writer: "Maybe it makes them respectable and a writer can't dare to be respectable" (Benson 796). John Steinbeck would finish *The Short Reign of Pippin IV* not for big sales, glowing reviews, or fawning prizes—he would do it for fun.

By November 1956 he finished the manuscript. The book came out in April 1957 and Viking's lack of enthusiasm translates in brief, curiously apologetic jacket copy: "It's clear that he [Steinbeck] has had a wonderful time writing it; and readers who don't hold it against a writer for changing his type will have a wonderful time reading it" (*Pippin*, original jacket). This less than rousing endorsement concludes: "On a different shelf from *Cannery Row* . . . and several aisles away from *The Grapes of Wrath*—it might find a place, we think, as a minor classic."

Steinbeck himself could have easily predicted the reviews, for they fell into the familiar pattern: some positive, some disappointed (fine book, but not up to *Grapes* form), some bewildered, and many downright negative. Probably the most astute of the contemporary reviews was from Elizabeth Janeway of the *New York Times Book Review*. Commenting on Steinbeck's "froth of a book," she concludes that "to insist on taking Mr. Steinbeck's fun too seriously is to be a spoilsport" (McElrath 431). Still, reviewer Fanny Butcher could not help responding to the jacket copy's hope of a "minor classic": "In this reader's opinion one of those last two words is superfluous, and that word isn't *minor*" (McElrath 430). One of the great surprises to result from the book's publication, at least to Steinbeck and Viking, was that it was selected by the Book-of-the-Month Club, assuring very good sales. However, Steinbeck was a brand name and releasing the book before the summer tourist season was a smart business move. As Janeway observes, "I am certain, that of next summer's crop of outward-bound American tourists, at least two-thirds will have with them a copy of *The Short Reign of Pippin IV*" (McElrath 431). Small wonder that an American tourist in France mistook Hemmingway for Steinbeck in 1959.

Steinbeck's light farce has received little attention from critics, compared to other works by the author. The major biographies by Benson and Jay Parini pass over the book quickly. "There is no plot to speak of," Parini writes, "the reader finds a loose assembly of episodes that spoof everything from French politics of the time to Texas millionaires to teenage girl novelists" (399). As Parini observes, the book's dependence on current affairs, shot through with Steinbeck's romantic, sentimental treatment "necessarily limits the appeal of *Pippin* for later readers" (399). Beginning with Peter Lisca's groundbreaking 1958 work, *The Wide World of John Steinbeck*, serious critics (and even supporters) of Steinbeck's work quickly pass over *Pippin*—wanting to forget it—or, as Lisca does, note the book as a signal of Steinbeck's artistic slide: "It is certain that the only interest in Steinbeck's last two books—*Sweet Thursday* and *The Short Reign of Pippin IV*—lies in their evidence of the author's present state of decline" (288). In subsequent essay collections on Steinbeck, however, *Sweet Thursday* receives considerably more attention than it had earlier. In recent, significant collections of essays on Steinbeck,[1] *Pippin* receives notice in a line or a paragraph but sometimes no mention at all. In sum, critics tend to dismiss the book as the lightest of Steinbeck's productions, perhaps a pale shadow of *Candide*, a time-bound farce without much bite as a satire, or a kind of way station for the decline-of-morality themes the author would take up more seriously in such works as *The Winter of Our Discontent* and *America and Americans*. Steinbeck's weak plotting, mundane style, and thin characters do not invite much discussion for good reason. A notable recent exception to this rule is Christine Rucklin's 2002 essay, "Beyond France: Steinbeck's *The Short Reign of Pippin IV*." She examines Steinbeck's careful review of French history as sources for the book, its resulting theme of historical events as cyclical (the brief return of the French monarchy), and the individual's struggle against the larger fate born of such cycles (Pippin does not want to be king but must temporarily endure his reign). Her observations are particularly interesting as Steinbeck politicizes the natural cycles that underpin earlier works such as *The Grapes of Wrath* or *To A God Unknown* (the individual's struggle against drought cycles, for example).

Perhaps the most valuable insights *The Short Reign of Pippin IV* provides to the contemporary critic or reader are insights into Steinbeck's comedic technique and his character as an artist. In *Pippin*, Steinbeck drew upon a lifetime of comic effects, upon every trick he had in his bag. Jackson Benson interviewed Steinbeck's third wife, Elaine, about the author's work on the book: "Elaine remembers that he never had more fun in his life. She could hear him while he was sitting at his table in the spare bedroom, chuckling and laughing while he wrote" (785). Whether critics and readers would appreciate it or not, Steinbeck pleased himself first with his employment of broad farce, satire, crude humor, puns, and irony (more specifically, his fascination with the paradoxes humans create for themselves).

Steinbeck's "fabrication" is a farce that skewers—rather too gently, as some critics observe—the chaotic state of French politics of the day and the insidious American tendency to commercialize everything, including the government of another country. Pippin Heristal faintly echoes the Steinbeck hero based on his friend, Edward F. Ricketts—a man of science (astronomy in this case), a kind of Renaissance man with a wide ranging curiosity who is interested in objective truth and therefore not in the day-to-day things that lack such truth: manners, popular culture, and especially politics. Mild counters to his sensibilities are his wife, Marie, who wishes to carefully manage a respectable household in middle-class fashion, and his daughter, Clotilde, who is obsessed with American culture and Hollywood. Pippin relies on advice from his Uncles Charles Martel, a politically cynical antiques dealer who, in typical Steinbeck fashion, is a good fellow but not above sales of dubious iniquities that might dupe the occasional rich rube. Marie goes to her friend, Sister Hyacinthe (Suzanne Lescault) for advice; another stock Steinbeck character, Hyacinthe is a former stripper who has become a nun simply because she is tired—her former irreverence masks a heart of gold. Once M. Rumorgue's Proto-Communist government fails, the National Assembly—beset with a dizzying array of competing political parties—finally elects to restore the French monarchy. As a descendent of Charlemagne, Pippin is named king, but he is the last to receive the news because he is much more interested in studying a meteor shower and in procuring a better camera to record it. Once the hapless Pippin is doomed to be king, he receives advice from Clotilde's American boyfriend, Tod Johnson, who is son of the "Egg King" of Petaluma, California. Johnson suggests adopting ideas from corporate America so that Pippin can more effectively run France. Miraculously, the French monarchy holds together for several months until Pippin actually tries to do something. Horrified that Pippin might be effective, the political parties turn on him and the French Republic, with all its chaos, is restored under the new government of M. Magot.

Though he was having fun, Steinbeck's humor in *Pippin* tends to be obvious or even juvenile. There are plenty of plays on names (Willie Chitling, a movie producer), crude jokes ("Her [Sister Hyacinthe's] bosom had remained high; her arches had fallen"), or distasteful episodes, as when Steinbeck mocks the speech of Duc des Troisfronts, who suffers from a cleft palate: "'I hive you the Hing of Fhance!'" (13, 136). Steinbeck's employment of his favorite comic device, pointing out paradoxical behavior, is the most sophisticated technique in *Pippin*, though it pales in comparison to its use in a much better novel, *Cannery Row*. Steinbeck was fascinated with paradox and, less than a decade after he wrote *Pippin*, he would write the chapter, "Paradox and Dream," as part of his explanation of American behavior in *America and Americans*: "Americans seem to live and breathe and function by paradox" (30). From the fictional political parties near the beginning of the novel (the Right or Left Centrists, the Christian Atheists) to the unease that emerges when the monarchy actually seems to work, *Pippin* derives much of its humor from the variety of paradoxes Steinbeck delights in pointing out. The heart of the novel's meaning, if there is one, occurs after Pippin has been accidentally banned from his palace at a time when he is not dressed like a king and, therefore, doesn't fit the preconceived notion of a king. Evicted from the palace grounds by a gardener and a gendarme, he buys a ticket and enters as a tourist. In a philosophical chat with Tod Johnson while drinking martinis, the two discuss the American corporations' fear of socialism while they themselves act like small socialist states. Johnson concludes, "'It's what you might call a paradox, sir.'" (90). When Pippin asks for an explanation, Johnson notes that the corporate ideal is undercut by "'circumstances and pressures'"—translated as the stated ideal runs into reality—but their discussion is cut off when Pippin is overcome by Johnson's martinis (90). Steinbeck's more complete consideration of paradox would have to wait for the chapter in *America and Americans*. The crowning paradox in Pippin comes when public unrest with the monarchy heightens as peace increases, and Heristal dooms himself by making a sensible speech before a gathering of French politicians and academics. The moment he appears to be a good leader, he is ousted.

As the original jacket copy suggests, for a better look at Steinbeck's effective use of humor, check another shelf for *Cannery Row*; for a better look at Steinbeck as a serious writer on weighty issues, go several aisles over for *The Grapes of Wrath*. For all of Viking's wishful thinking at the time, *The Short Reign of Pippin IV* will never be considered a classic, not even a minor one. Arguably, it is the weakest book Steinbeck published. The existence of *Pippin*, however, is most intriguing as a window into Steinbeck's attitude toward his art.

Written on ledger pages facing each day's work while he was writing *East of Eden* and later collected in a book, *Journal of a Novel: The East of Eden Letters*, Steinbeck's letters to Pascal Covici staked out his territory as an adventurous, even risk-taking author: "A good writer always works at the impossible. There is another kind who pulls in his horizons . . . and giving up the impossible he gives up writing. . . . this has not happened to me" (4). Later, responding to Covici's criticism of recent submissions from the *East of Eden* manuscript, Steinbeck angrily wrote, "You said this morning you had to sell x thousands of copies [but] I am sure, after all of our years together, you will not ask me to make one single change for the sake of sales except in terms of clarity" (55). Steinbeck was not a writer who sought fame or money or critical accolades. He wrote where the work took him, no matter the risk to reputation or sales—as was the case with *Pippin*. Concluding his own "rationale" for his work as a writer, Steinbeck wrote, "My work is and has been fun. Within myself, I find no hunger to inquire further" (Shillinglaw 162).

Ernest Hemingway might have found Steinbeck's wide open, "fun" writing aestheticly baffling and, therefore, his response to *Pippin* as a kind of authorial toe jam is not surprising. Two and a half years after Hemingway wrote those remarks about *Pippin*, he committed suicide at his home in Ketchum on July 2, 1961. In a letter to Covici, Steinbeck was baffled—not believing that a hunter of Hemingway's skill could have died in a gun-cleaning accident, as the press reported—and ultimately saddened by his perception of Hemingway as an artist: "He has not a vestige of humor. . . . Always he tried to prove something. He was the critics' darling because he never changed style, theme nor story. He made no experiments in thinking nor in emotion" (Steinbeck, *Letters*,

704). Steinbeck finally summed up Hemingway in a paradox: "He really cared about his immortality as though he weren't sure of it. And there's little doubt that he has it" (704). Steinbeck himself, if he cared at all, would reserve "immortality" for his big books, like *The Grapes of Wrath* or his personal favorite, *East of Eden*. He looked upon the short, happy life of *Pippin* as the grand joke that it was meant to be. He would have likely told the critics of the future that they should peruse the aisles for *The Grapes of Wrath* or *Cannery Row* if they wished, but that a book like *The Short Reign of Pippin IV* did not deserve a place on the shelves at all.

NOTE

1. Such collections include *Steinbeck's Typewriter: Essays on His Art* (1996), *Steinbeck and the Environment* (1997), two centennial tributes to Steinbeck (one edited by Stephen K. George [2002] and one by Syed Mashkoor Ali [2004]), and a book in which Steinbeck's political viewpoint may be considered, again edited by Stephen K. George—*The Moral Philosophy of John Steinbeck* (2005).

WORKS CITED

Ali, Syed Mashkoor, ed. *John Steinbeck: A Centennial Tribute*. Jaipur, India: Surabhi Publications, 2004.

Beegel, Susan F., Susan Shillinglaw, and Wesley N. Tiffney, Jr. *Steinbeck and the Environment*. Tuscaloosa: University of Alabama Press, 1997.

Benson, Jackson J. *The True Adventures of John Steinbeck, Writer*. New York: Viking, 1984.

DeMott, Robert. *Steinbeck's Typewriter: Essays on His Art*. Troy, NY: Whitston Publishing Company, 1996.

George, Stephen K., ed. *The Moral Philosophy of John Steinbeck*. Lanham, MD: Scarecrow Press, 2005.

——, ed. *John Steinbeck: A Centennial Tribute*. Westport, CT: Praeger, 2002.

Hemingway, Ernest. *Selected Letters, 1917–1961*. Ed. Carlos Baker. New York: Scribners, 1981.

Hemingway, Valerie. *Running with the Bulls: My Years with the Hemingways*. New York: Ballantine Books, 2004.

Lisca, Peter. *The Wide World of John Steinbeck*. Brunswick, NJ: Rutgers University Press, 1958.

McElrath, Joseph R., Jr., Jesse S. Crisler, and Susan Shillinglaw, eds. *John Steinbeck: The Contemporary Reviews.* Cambridge, UK: Cambridge University Press, 1996.

Parini, Jay. *John Steinbeck: A Biography.* New York: Henry Holt, 1995.

Rucklin, Christine. "Beyond France, Steinbeck's *The Short Reign of Pippin IV.*" *Beyond Boundaries: Rereading John Steinbeck.* Eds. Susan Shillinglaw and Kevin Hearle. Tuscaloosa: University of Alabama Press, 2002. 162–70.

Steinbeck, John. *America and Americans.* New York: Viking, 1966.

———. *Journal of a Novel, The* East of Eden *Letters.* New York: Viking, 1969.

———. "Rationale." *America and Americans and Selected Nonfiction.* Eds. Susan Shillinglaw and Jackson J. Benson. New York: Viking, 2002. 161–62.

Steinbeck, John. *The Short Reign of Pippin IV.* (Jacket Copy.) New York: Viking, 1957.

———. *The Short Reign of Pippin IV.* 1957. New York: Penguin, 1977.

———. *Steinbeck: A Life in Letters.* Eds. Elaine Steinbeck and Robert Wallsten. 1975. New York: Penguin, 1989.

14

"Fingers of Cloud: A Satire on College Protervity"

A Meditative Reading

Kiyoshi Nakayama
Kansai University

In 1919 John Steinbeck graduated from the Salinas High School and entered Stanford University. He studied intermittently at Palo Alto, belonged to the English Club, made many good friends, and for the first time in February and May, 1924, published the short stories "Fingers of Cloud: A Satire on College Protervity" and "Adventures in Arcademy: A Journey into the Ridiculous," respectively, in the monthly magazine *Stanford Spectator*. Steinbeck portrayed in "Fingers of Cloud," for the first time and the last, Filipino farmhands who work on a sugar beet ranch, in particular featuring a young boss of the Filipino group who marries a white girl.

The subtitle of the story "A Satire on College Protervity" is somehow mysterious in that the story has nothing to do with college life except that it was published in the monthly magazine *Stanford Spectator* in February, 1924. Since the word "protervity" basically means "peevishness," the story may connote a satire on the feminine protagonist who is short-tempered and peevish, though she is not a college student. The story begins with Gertie's sweeping the porch:

> Gertie swept all of the dirt to the largest crack in the floor of the porch. Several times she went back to gather up bits that had escaped the flat side of the broom. Then she very carefully edged the line of dust to the

crack and tumbled it over, chuckling gaily while she swept briskly at
imaginary particles.

"Last time, last time—shan't ever do it again—last time—last time."
She ended with a little shriek and a vicious stab at the receiving crack.
The broom sailed into the house, popped against a wall, and the door
slammed after it. Gertie flounced her skirt and sat down on the top step,
her voice continuing at a monotonous sing-song.

"Ma's gone—Ma's gone—and she ain't comin' back no more," and
mixed with a giggle—"this is the best fun since Pa didn't come back.
Wish't Ma belonged to a lodge," and a businesslike chant—"Don't have
to sweep no more—don't have to wash no more—don't have to do ab-
so-lute-ly nothin' no more." The "no more" was working itself into a
refrain. Again she ended with a little shriek of pleasure. . . . (149)

Here, the reader finds that Gertie feels happy at her mother's death
and that her father had died or disappeared long before the mother
died. Why Gertie feels pleasure seems simple, as she says: "Don't have
to sweep no more—don't have to wash no more—don't have to do
ab-so-lute-ly nothin' no more." Thus, the repetition of "last time" and
"no more" is a characteristic feature of the story—providing a poetic,
ballad-like tone. The narrator underscores this repetitious, echoing
tone by commenting that "the 'no more' was working itself into a
refrain" (149). (This ballad-like device Steinbeck will later employ to
great effect in *Of Mice and Men*.)

Another interesting feature of the story is a possible rationale underlying Gertie and her speech habits. First, by naming her "Gertie,"
the young Steinbeck may have been an oblique reference to Gertrude
Stein, a well-known modernist writer whose effective use of repetition was notable. Second, Gertie's shrieks, giggles, and repetition of
phrases portray character—reflecting both an emotional disconnect in
her indifference about her mother's death and her father's disappear-
ance and her limited intelligence.

Incidentally, Peter Lisca introduces this story as "an account of a
subnormal girl who marries a migrant Filipino laborer," adding that
"this odd mixture of the realistic and the fantastic is even more pro-
nounced in the other story, 'Adventures in Arcademy: A Journey into
the Ridiculous,' an obscure and satirical allegory of college life at Stanford" (24). Following Lisca's contention, John H. Timmerman regards
Gertie as "a half-witted orphan" (13). The narrator's description gives
the impression that she is white:

On her flat pink face there was a benign smile that seemed glued on;
her hair, white as a washed sheep's wool and nearly as curly, bobbed

knowingly on the top of her head, and her pink eyes blandly regarded everything on the street. (149)

Eighteen years old and an orphan, she wades across the river and starts up "a little hill which pretended to be a mountain" (149).

There follows a fantastic scene reminiscent of *Alice in Wonderland* in which Gertie converses with the yellow May-flowers blooming on the hill.

> The slope was carpeted with the palest green of early spring. Some yellow May-flowers peeked from under their leaves and said,
> "Boo! You are running away, my girl." Gertie stopped and regarded them fiercely.
> "I am not running away. I guess I'm eighteen and know my own mind. Besides, I'm an orphant, and an orphant can't run away because she ain't got absolutely nothing to run away from." She trampled the flowers into the ground and pranced on. On top of the foolish little mountain she sat down to watch the autos crawl along the highway. A faint echo of their horns came to her from below. Now and then there would be a blinding flash as the sun found a windshield. (149)

When the flowers criticize Gertie, she flares up, tramples them into the ground, and prances on to the top of the mountain. Once on top of the hill, she sits down to watch the autos crawl along the highway. Thus, the reader finds, as another characteristic of the story, the fantastic scene and the realistic description juxtaposed in a paragraph.

Here at the starting point of her new life as a wanderer, the narrator portrays Gertie's desire to watch or possibly to touch the clouds as the title of the story suggests:

> The clouds had been up here when she was below. She had rather bargained on touching them, but now they had jumped higher than she could reach. Lying down, she could better watch them hurrying along. A big grey one brushed her eyelids with its hanging shreds until they closed; a smaller one rushed up and pressed gently, and she slept." (149)

Her playing with the clouds is like a flash forward to the scene in "The Great Mountains" of *The Red Pony*, in which Jody Tifflin plays with the clouds moving over a ridge of the Santa Lucia Mountains:

> Then [Jody] lay on his back in the grass and looked up at the dumpling summer clouds. By closing one eye and destroying perspective he brought them down within reach so that he could put up his fingers and stroke them. He helped the gentle wind push them down the sky; it

seemed to him that they went faster for his help. One fat white cloud he
helped clear to the mountain rims and pressed firmly over, out of sight.
Jody wondered what it was seeing, then." (176)

This desire to live close to nature is one of the quintessential characteristics of Steinbeck's work. Among other characters who reflect this
quality, for example, Helen Van Deventer in *The Pastures of Heaven*
comes to the village to live in a beautiful community surrounded by
nature, which she believes has healing properties.

That Gertie has an urge to be a bum is likewise a flash forward to
a continuing theme—this time to Steinbeck admiration of the bum's
way of life in *The Wayward Bus* and later in *Travels with Charley in
Search of America*. The attention-starved wife, Elisa Allen, in "The
Chrysanthemums" yearns for the itinerant tinker's wandering way of
life. As she watches his wagon crawling along the river, she whispers:
"That's a bright direction. There's a glowing there" (14). Timmerman
also recognizes a poignant similarity between Gertie and Elisa:

> One also senses in Gertie a character and theme that would emerge more
> powerfully several years later in the portrait of Elisa Allen of 'The Chry-
> santhemums.' Gertie possesses the same powerful longing for freedom,
> and the compulsion to pursue her dreams." (12)

Steinbeck's admiration for the bum's way of life includes as well an
admiration for laziness, which he considers a virtue contrary to "busy-
ness [which] is merely a kind of nervous tic" (*The Log* 182).

Unfortunately, the peacefulness of Gertie's temporary rest at the
top of the hill ends when a downpour awakens her, forcing her to
run down the hill to find a shelter. On the other side of the hill, she
finds a bunkhouse where Filipino farmhands live, which she calls a
"foreign camp." As Nelson Valjean suggests in *The Errant Knight*, the
place looks very much like the bunkhouse Steinbeck describes in *Of
Mice and Men* (73–74)—another flash forward to works yet to come:

> The Filipinos sat on the floor with their feet under them. From the out-
> side the howling wind came through the cracks in the house and made
> the burlap hangings move restlessly. Burlap tacked loosely on the walls,
> a littered floor of dust-colored wood, a few boxes to sit on, and the fat-
> bellied stove, that was the lounging room of the bunkhouse. Three of
> the pock-marked brown men played cards on the floor under a coal oil
> lamp. They threw down their cards without a word. No one was talking
> in the room. Ten or twelve more of the squatty figures were dumped

about the room, half smiling because there would be no work in the beet fields the next day. (149)

Twelve or thirteen men live together in the bunkhouse, and Pedro, as the boss, provides payment, food, clothing, and shelter. Since it is raining hard, one of the card-playing men jeers, "Hee! Pedro is not so happy tonight. He loses money tomorrow. We eat and we do not work" (149).

Parenthetically, Steinbeck will later discuss Filipinos and their relationship to women in his essay, "Always Something to Do in Salinas"—reminiscent also of the paucity of women and the whorehouses in *Of Mice and Men*:

> The need for labor became great. We brought in Filipinos to cut and chop the lettuce and there were interesting results. No Filipino women were allowed in and the dark, quick little men constantly got into trouble with what were called "white women." The Filipinos lived and worked in clots of five or six. If you had a fight with one, you had six on you. They bought automobiles cooperatively by clots and got women the same way. The wages of five or six mounted up and they could afford to buy themselves a pretty fair communal woman. For some reason this outraged the tender morals of certain of our citizens who didn't seem to be morally sensitive in other directions. There used to be some pretty fine gang fights in the pool rooms of Market Street of a Saturday night. (58)

Into just such a cooperative "clot" Gertie will arrive. But before she arrives at the bunkhouse, while she is making her way down the hill, a bootlegger, "a large red man" with red hair and red face, visits the bunkhouse to sell his whisky. While he talks and drinks some of his sample whisky as demonstration, Pedro signals for Manuel to sneak out of the house to steal some bottles. Not realizing that all of his merchandise has been stolen, the red man leaves. The Filipinos consume the whisky very quickly.

As Pedro drinks from the bottle, they hear, together with the sound of the wind, something like the sound of a coyote outside the house. Pedro goes to see what is making the sound even though the oldest man warns, "Pedro, you must not go—Pedro, do you hear? It is the Kari, Pedro—She eats the wet brains of the new-buried dead, and she crazes those who see her—Pedro, I command you not to go" (162). Though there is no evidence of this Filipino evil spirit, the Kari here seems to be similar to an Indian goddess Kali, Shiva's wife, a vicious figure.

Pedro finds Gertie "blanketed with caked mud" (162), grasps her under the arm, and drags her near to the fire. Then he kindly gives her a basin of cold water to wash herself and brings a blanket so that she may kick off her wet dress. Then Pedro croons to her, "I give you my bed in a room where no one is. There you may rest" (162). Gertie nods absently, responding, "Yeh! and I'm about ready for it, too" (162). Pedro leads her into a tiny closet where there is room only for the narrow cot. In contrast, later in *Of Mice and Men*, the farmhands live in a bunkhouse with bunks positioned around the walls. Here in the bunkhouse in the short story, everyone may have his own closet.

Before Pedro leaves the closet, he looks long at her, and then she smiles at him, showing her teeth. The effect on Pedro is instantaneous:

> Pedro went out feeling attractive and warm and dizzy. In the outer room he looked at the men superciliously. He wanted to maintain the glory he had gained in going to meet the Kari even if it had not been the Kari. "I am going to marry the woman." He hardly noticed the words he used. (162)

At Pedro's formidable statement, one of the men laughs, and the oldest jeers, "'Hee! you fool, . . . They do not marry us, they will not marry us, and you are a fool'" (162). But Pedro proudly answers, "'You have not seen many like me. I say that I am going to marry the woman. She will marry me, for I know of woman; I have known of woman nearly as white as this one'" (162–63). And Pedro returns to the closet in which Gertie is sleeping. The narrator describes the ensuing scene:

> He was a little frightened at the job he had undertaken. Gertie started up at his entrance. He sat on the side of bed and looked into her eyes. She was fascinated by the satiny texture of his eyes. They bit into her stomach and sent rivers of fire through her veins. Her body jerked convulsively, and, throwing her arms about his neck, she kissed him thickly on the lips. (163)

The next morning Pedro and Gertie go to town to get married—an action as impetuous as that of Curley and his wife in *Of Mice and Men*. Curley's wife confesses to Lennie: "So I married Curley. Met him out to the Riverside Dance Palace that same night" (86). Both couples were similarly impulsive and thoughtless. Living in a small house across from the bunkhouse, as time goes by, Gertie

> had become a queen among the brown men. Her meals were brought to her on a steaming platter, potatoes and brown gravy and stew. And

Pedro was constantly busy keeping her fame inviolate, for in it lay his claim to greatness. She was very workless and very happy. (163)

Since Pedro is able to monopolize a white woman by the means of matrimony, he has to keep his eyes open lest she be seduced by someone else. Here, however, the story reaches its highest development:

The summer heat irritated Pedro. . . . The yellow ground and the dun grass threw all of the heat of the sun back into the air. On an evening when his back was sweaty he beat Gertie with a curtain rod. She whimpered and discovered that he was very black, but she stored the knowledge for future use. (163)

The heat contributes to Pedro's fury and mindlessness as he beats his wife—the kind of violence that might occur in everyday life in the Filipines, where Pedro had been born. Gertie just whimpers, but discovers that he is very black.

Although she has lichi nuts and rock candy the next day to pay for her beating, Pedro remains a bully and black. She can forgive him for this blackness:

"Pedro, you're awful black, an' I'm white." The heat and some small work had ruined Pedro.

"Yes, you too white—you white all over—no black hair, why not?"

"Well! I haven't got any dirty half-white holes in my face from smallpox like some people I know, and besides white's a good color. All white folks are—white, an' I'm white, an' you're terrible black."

Pedro was very silent and hurt, and she was made brave. "I don't think I'm goin' to stay with you very long, 'cause you're black, see!" (163)

Gertie's declaration that "white's a good color" and that she is not going to stay with Pedro very long because he is black reveals a hatred of blackness and a sense of the racial superiority of whites. Pedro listens with no retort or protest. Looking at her with disgust, he "climbed into bed in a way which made Gertie sleep on the floor"—a position implying that their marital life has ended.

The next day when the heat becomes unbearable, Gertie wants to cool herself by standing in the fire barrel, with the water to her waist, squatting so that she will be covered to her neck. But when she lifts the lid, she starts back in amazement: "Floating in the water there were three horses' heads. The flesh was partly gone; where eyes should have been were black holes, the nose bones stuck out and the cheeks were gone entirely" (164). She is furious, of course, though she has no idea why the horses' heads are stored in the fire barrel. According to Jeffrey Schultz and Luchen Li in their *Critical Companion to John Steinbeck*, horses' heads are kept in a barrel "to scare off evil spirits"—it is a matter of superstition (84).

Superstition has surrounded Pedro and Gertie's relationship from the beginning. All of the Filipinos regard her as the Kari before she even appears—a superstition Pedro fondly accepts even after their marriage, often muttering "that she was indeed the Kari" (163). Here lies a deep cultural gap between the Filipino and the American, and Gertie is not tolerant of the Flipino's superstition. Another serious quarrel ensues:

> If Pedro had been wise, he would have wiped his back that night. Gertie was tired of sleeping on the floor, and when he came in with his wet back, her temper burst out.
>
> "Say you! There's horses' heads in the fire barrel, an' I won't have it. I say I won't have them in there, and you see that you take every single one out right straight. Think I'm goin' to live in a place where they keep horses' heads in their fire barrel? No, sir!" Pedro squirmed guiltily. He had known something of the sort would happen. (164)

But Pedro is not wise, and his back is wet with sweat—repellent to his wife. There is neither understanding nor love between them, and she has come to view him as "the other." To Gertie's diatribe, Pedro responds defensively, maintaining that

> "those other men, they do it. I cannot stop. Boss say, no more horse head in fire barrel, but those men still do put them. Why you care for horse head if top on barrel? I think I buy blue dress for you. You like?'" (164)

But Gertie will not listen to him:

> "Now you listen here, you black runt, you. . . . I don't want them horse heads, and the sooner you understand it the better. Just you keep on knowing that I won't have horse heads. . . . An' besides, your back is always, always, so damned sweaty!" (164)

On a summer's day, Gertie, lured by the clouds playing about slowly on top of the mountain, leaves Pedro without saying goodbye. She climbs barefoot through the grass, chanting:

"No more, no more, I ain't coming down no more. I just won't absolutely live with him no more if he thinks more of his old horses' heads
than he does of me. I ain't coming back no more. I'll live up there in the
sun." She quickened her steps and mounted very rapidly. In a moment
she started to run, and she was breathless when she came to the top.

Suddenly she realized that the clouds had jumped up a long way. She
was as angry as her breathlessness would permit. From the highway below,
though, came the occasional honk of an automobile horn, and now and
then, there was a blinding flash as the sun found a windshield. (164)

Unable to play with the clouds as she had hoped, instead she watches
the cars clawing along the highway. This is another beginning of her
life as wanderer.

The topography for the locale of the mountain Gertie climbs is
assumed to be the top of the south side hill of Samuel Hamilton's
ranch, later described in *East of Eden* and located in the southern
suburbs of King City, from which Route 198 running from San Lucas
to the Central Valley in the east is clearly seen below. I happened to
stand there twice when I visited the Hamilton ranch in 1992 and 2003
(the ranch was sold in 1914 and Ernest and Bonnie Grab owned it in
2003), and was impressed at the sight of automobiles moving along
the highway in the distance as though they were crawling. Since the
Salinas River runs close to King City, the reader may imagine that
Gertie crosses it twice, as though she symbolically goes over to the
other side of the world.

The locale of the beet farm where Pedro and his men worked may
be considered to be the Rancho San Lorenzo in the north of the King
City which Claus Spreckels purchased from Charles King in 1897,
when Spreckels came to the Salinas Valley to start building his five-
story sugar factory in the suburbs of Salinas (Fink 163). Young Steinbeck often had temporary jobs at the factory and in one of the Spreckels Ranches in the Salinas Valley. In the fall of 1920, for instance, he
was hired as straw boss at the ranch near Chualar, about ten miles
south of Salinas. Considering Steinbeck's propensity to draw on personal experience, in all likelihood he drew on his own observations
in "Fingers of Cloud."

The ethnic and multicultural aspects of Steinbeck Country are fully
delineated in the story, with conversations between Gertie and Pedro
in a colloquial vernacular typical of the area. Similar colloquial usage
occurs in *Of Mice and Men*. Very often Pedro's speech is imperfect, in
so-called pidgin English.

Steinbeck portrayed Pedro as the other—one of those savage, superstitious Filipinos imported to the United States in the 1920s—one who doesn't wipe sweat off of his back and who sometimes beats a woman when irritated by the heat. Gertie marries Pedro, lured by his initial kind gestures and satin eyes, but she leaves him because of her hatred of the color of his skin and his superstitious behavior. The differences between the two cultures are so wide and deep that they are unable to live together as in a fairy tale romance.

Steinbeck portrays Gertie and Pedro's inability to understand one another—their inability to share cultures and traditions honestly even though they get married. His short story, then, is social criticism through a satire on "College Protervity," which includes a matter of women's liberation and longing for freedom from social restraint in an age of a patriarchal society. Later, in 1937, Steinbeck would poignantly explore the same theme in the character of Elisa Allen in a more widely read and admired short story, "The Chrysanthemums."

WORKS CITED

Fink, Augusta. *Monterey: The Presence of the Past.* San Francisco: Chronicle Books, 1972.

Hughes, Robert S., Jr. *Beyond* The Red Pony: *A Reader's Companion to Steinbeck's Complete Short Stories.* Metuchen, NJ: Scarecrow Press, 1987

Lisca, Peter. *The Wide World of John Steinbeck.* New Brunswick, NJ: Rutgers University Press, 1958.

Schultz, Jeffrey, and Luchen Li, eds. *Critical Companion to John Steinbeck: A Literary Reference to His Life and Work.* New York: Checkmark Books, 2005.

Steinbeck, John. "Always Something to Do in Salinas." *Holiday* 17.6 (June 1955): 58–59, 152–53, 156.

———. "Fingers of Cloud: A Satire on College Protervity." *Stanford Spectator* Vol. 2 (Feb. 1924): 149, 161–64.

———. *The Log from the Sea of Cortez.* 1951. New York: Viking, 1969.

———. *The Long Valley.* 1938. New York: Penguin Books, 1995.

———. *Of Mice and Men.* 1937. New York: Penguin Books, 1995.

———. *The Pastures of Heaven.* 1932. New York: Penguin Books, 1995.

Timmerman, John H. *The Dramatic Landscape of Steinbeck's Short Stories.* Norman: University of Oklahoma Press, 1990.

Valjean, Nelson. *John Steinbeck: The Errant Knight.* San Francisco: Chronicle Books, 1975.

Index

About the Contributors

Mary M. Brown teaches literature and creative writing at Indiana Wesleyan University and chairs the Division of Modern Language, Literature, and Communication. She writes poetry, essays, and criticism in modern and contemporary American literature. She loves the work of John Steinbeck and remembers with gratitude and fondness the gracious and collegial spirit of Stephen George.

Danica Cerce is assistant professor of American literature at the University of Ljubljana, Slovenia, and is presently teaching English for the Faculty of Economics. She received a Ph.D. in literary sciences in May 2002 and an M.A. in Australian literature in 1995, both from the Faculty of Arts, University of Ljubljana. She has given papers on Steinbeck in Slovenia, the United States, and Japan and has contributed several articles for various academic and literary journals at home and abroad. She is author of *Pripovednistvo Johna Steinbecka* (*The Narrative Prose of John Steinbeck*) (2006), based on her doctoral dissertation.

Stephen K. George was a professor of English at Brigham Young University–Idaho. He edited *John Steinbeck: A Centennial Tribute* and *The Moral Philosophy of John Steinbeck* and was co-editor of *John Steinbeck and His Contemporaries*. In addition, he wrote dozens of articles and reviews. At the time of his death, Stephen was co-editor of the *Steinbeck Review* and co-director of the Steinbeck Society of America. He was director of Brigham Young University–Idaho's literary journal, *Outlet*, and, until his death, resided with his family in the quiet town of Rexburg, Idaho.

Mimi Reisel Gladstein is president of the John Steinbeck Society of America. Her book, *The Indestructible Woman in Faulkner, Hemingway, and Steinbeck*, and her many articles in scholarly anthologies and journals evidence her myriad and varied approaches to Steinbeck studies. Gladstein has received both the Burkhardt Award for Research and the John J. and Angeline Pruis Award for Teaching Steinbeck. The University of Texas at El Paso has recognized her with the 2006 Distinguished Achievement Award for Service to Students and the 1988 Burlington Northern Award for Teaching Excellence. In 2003 she was honored with the Outstanding Faculty Achievement Award in the College of Liberal Arts. Gladstein, a pioneer in women's studies, is listed in *Feminists Who Changed America, 1963–75*.

Charlotte Hadella is Professor of English and writing in the Department of Language, Literature, and Philosophy at Southern Oregon University. She teaches courses in American literature, young adult literature, and English education. She also directs the Oregon Writing Project at SOU. Her Steinbeck scholarship includes the Twayne Masterworks Series book *Of Mice and Men: A Kinship of Powerlessness*, as well as numerous articles on the fiction of John Steinbeck.

Tetsumaro Hayashi, professor emeritus of Ball State University, also served as graduate professor of English and vice president and director of graduate studies at Yasuda Women's University in Hiroshima and was former president of the International John Steinbeck Society (1981–93). Dr. Hayashi has published thirty-four books and twenty-three monographs on British and American literature. He was editor-in-chief of *Steinbeck Quarterly* (1968–93) and the Steinbeck Monograph Series (1970–91) while at Ball State University in Muncie, Indiana.

Luchen Li is associate professor of humanities and director of the Office of International Programs at Kettering University in Flint, Michigan. His recent achievements include co-editing *John Steinbeck's Global*

Dimensions (2008), editing *John Steinbeck: A Documentary* (2005), and co-authoring *Critical Companion to John Steinbeck: A Literary Reference to His Life and Work* (2005). He served on the editorial board for Stephen George's book *The Moral Philosophy of John Steinbeck* and presently serves on the editorial board for the *Steinbeck Review*. He is also vice president of international relations for the John Steinbeck Society of America.

Michael J. Meyer is adjunct professor of English at DePaul and Northeastern Illinois Universities in Chicago. He is the current Steinbeck bibliographer, and his essays on Steinbeck have appeared in numerous books and journals. He edited *Cain Sign: The Betrayal of Brotherhood in the Work of John Steinbeck* and is presently working on literature and music titles for Rodopi Press's series *Perspectives in Modern Literature*. He is also co-editor of the *Steinbeck Encyclopedia*.

Kiyoshi Nakayama is professor of English at Kumamoto Gakuen University and the current president of the John Steinbeck Society of Japan (2002–present). He is the author of more than fifty articles on teaching English and twentieth-century American literature, as well as twenty-five books, nineteen of which are on or relating to John Steinbeck. Among them is a trilogy of critical studies written in Japanese: *John Steinbeck's Writings: The California Years* (1989), *The Post-California Years* (1999), and *The New York Years* (2002). He is compiler of *Steinbeck in Japan: A Bibliography* (1992), co-editor of *John Steinbeck: Asian Perspectives* (1992), co-translator of Steinbeck's *Sweet Thursday* (1984) and *To a God Unknown* (2001), and translator of *The Grapes of Wrath* (1997) into Japanese. He was awarded the Richard W. and Dorothy Burkhardt Award for outstanding contribution to Steinbeck criticism in 1992 and the John J. and Angelina R. Pruis Award in 2002.

Brian Railsback is professor of English and founding dean of the Honors College at Western Carolina University. His previous books include *Parallel Expeditions: Charles Darwin and the Art of John Steinbeck* (1995) and *A John Steinbeck Encyclopedia* (2006), co-edited with Michael J. Meyer. A member of the editorial board of the *Steinbeck Review*, Professor Railsback has published numerous articles and book chapters on John Steinbeck and lectured on the author in Japan, Mexico, and the United States.

Thom Satterlee teaches creative writing at Taylor University in Upland, Indiana. His poetry has appeared in *Alaska Quarterly Review*, *Crazyhorse*, *Image*, *Notre Dame Review*, *Southern Review*, and *Southwest Review* and has been selected for inclusion in *Poetry Daily* three times. His first collection, *Burning Wyclif* (2006), was an American Library Association Notable Book and a finalist for the 2007 *L.A. Times* Book Prize in Poetry.

Stephen L. Tanner is Ralph A. Britsch Humanities Professor of English Emeritus at Brigham Young University. He is author of four books and numerous articles and chapters of literary biography and criticism. He received the Lionel Trilling award for distinguished literary criticism. He has published frequently on American fiction of the twentieth century.

John H. Timmerman, professor of English at Calvin College in Grand Rapids, Michigan, has published two books and many essays on John Steinbeck. Additionally, during the past decade he has published *T. S. Eliot: The Poetics of Recovery*, *Jane Kenyon: A Literary Life*, and *Robert Frost: The Ethics of Ambiguity*.

About the Editor

Barbara A. Heavilin currently serves, with Paul Douglass of the Steinbeck Center at San Jose, as co-editor of the *Steinbeck Review*, now a part of Blackwell's American Author Series. She also edited the *Steinbeck Yearbook* (2000–2004), which appeared in three volumes as a hardcover collection of essays and served as a bridge from the *Steinbeck Quarterly* to the *Review*. Along with Stephen K. George, she is co-founder of the *Steinbeck Review* and the New Steinbeck Society of America. She served as co-director of the "Steinbeck and His Contemporaries" conference.

Heavilin has published numerous articles and books on John Steinbeck, including *The Critical Response to John Steinbeck's* The Grapes of Wrath (2000), *John Steinbeck's* The Grapes of Wrath: *A Reference Guide* (2002), and *John Steinbeck's* Of Mice and Men: *A Reference Guide* (2005). She is also editor, with her husband, of *The Quaker Presence in America* (2003) and has published articles and reviews on Margaret Fell Fox, William Wordsworth, and James Thurber. She has been awarded the Pruis Award for outstanding contributions to Steinbeck studies and teaches Restoration and eighteenth-century British literature, world literature, and linguistics and grammar—among other subjects—at Taylor University.